Poverty, crime and punishment

Dee Cook

CPAG Ltd, 1-5 Bath Street, Lon

CPAG promotes action for the relief, directly or indirectly, of poverty among children and families with children. We work to ensure that those on low incomes get their full entitlements to welfare benefits. In our campaigning and information work we seek to improve benefits and policies for low-income families, in order to eradicate the injustice of poverty. If you are not already supporting us, please consider making a donation, or ask for details of our membership schemes and publications.

Poverty Publication 97

Published by CPAG Ltd
1-5 Bath Street, London EC1V 9PY

© CPAG Ltd 1997

ISBN 0 946744 97 1

The views expressed in this book are the author's and are not necessarily those of CPAG.

The cartoon on p139 is © Cole/The Sunday Times, 11 July 1993.

A CIP record for this book is available from the British Library

Cover and design by Devious Designs 0114 275 5634
Cover photographs Format Photographers and the Guardian
Typeset by Nancy White 0171 607 4510
Printed by Progressive Printing UK Ltd 01702 520050

CONTENTS

ACKNOWLEDGEMENTS   vii

FOREWORD Michael Mansfield QC   ix

1 POVERTY AND CRIME: THE SAME OLD STORY?   1
   Introduction   1
   Talk about crime and poverty   1
   The 'dishonest' poor   3
   Crime, morality and the 'underclass'   5
   Poverty, de-moralisation and blame   7
   Re-moralisation and the 'new rabble'   8
   Crime and 'problem families'   11
   Crime and locality: 'problem' areas   14
   Summary   17

2 POVERTY, INEQUALITY AND CRIME   21
   Introduction   21
   Poverty – what poverty?   22
   The legacy of Thatcherism   23
   The 'haves' and the 'have nots'   26
   Poverty, citizenship and social exclusion   28
   The rights and duties of the 'good citizen'   30
   Marginalisation and relative deprivtion   31
   Does unemployment cause crime?   32
   Crimes of poverty: prostitution   36
   Crimes of poverty: social security fraud   38
   Summary   40

3 CRIME PROBLEMS   43
   Introduction: what is crime?   43
   Official statistics: what counts as crime?   45
   Crime trends: what do we think we know about crime?   48
   What don't we know about crime and punishment?   53

Hidden crimes: domestic violence and racial harassment 55
Missing crimes 59
Summary: some alternative crime 'problems' 64

4 POVERTY, PUNISHMENT AND JUSTICE **69**
Introduction 69
Wealth, poverty and the criminal justice process 70
External factors shaping criminal justice 75
Offender-related factors shaping criminal justice 77
Who gets punished and why? 83
Who is the indentikit prisoner? 86
What is prison for? 89
Does punishment reduce crime – does prison work? 90
Poverty, unemployment and imprisonment –
    managing problem populations 92
Does crime and punishment pay? 93

5 CRIME, NEED AND GREED **99**
Give and take 100
One law for the rich? 101
The politics of 'scrounging' 106
Taxation, welfare and getting elected 107
Hotlines and billboard politics 109
Fraud campaigns 110
Rights, duties and individual responsibility 112
Targeting 'fraud-prone' groups 114
Summary 116

6 POVERTY AND VICTIMISATION **118**
Introduction 118
Patterns of victimisation: the British Crime Survey, 1996 119
Patterns of victimisation: the Wolverhampton Crime Audit 121
Crime, anxiety and locality 124
Hidden victims 127
The 'myth of the equal victim' 127

7 SOCIAL POLICY, CRIME AND PUNISHMENT **131**
Introduction 131
Immigration policy and the policing of visible minorities 132
Lone parent families 136
'Problem' youth 143

The homeless and beggars: zero tolerance?   149
Summary   152

8 CONCLUSIONS   **155**
Crime: who suffers?   155
Crime: who benefits?   155
De-moralisation   156
Poverty, crime and punishment – complicating the picture   157
Social policy and crime – turning the tables   160
Where to start?   163

APPENDIX 1: Social deprivation indices   165

APPENDIX 2: A note on 'ethnic minority' classifications   166

ACKNOWLEDGEMENTS

I owe many people many thanks for their help in the production of this book. Thanks to Peter Golding who, as Chair of CPAG's publications committee, first suggested the project to me and to Frances Ellery, CPAG publications officer and the book's editor, for her patience, support and commitment. Thanks are also due to Frances and to Carey Oppenheim and Jon Vagg for reading the manuscript and for giving me such positive and helpful comments. I am also grateful to friends and colleagues (especially Jo Phoenix and Martin Roberts) who allowed me to draw upon their research and their considerable expertise; to Maggie McAndrew and the Wolverhampton Community Safety Partnership who commissioned the Wolverhampton Crime Audit; and to Adrian Sinfield for his advice and encouragement.

On a personal note, this book has been written despite a series of domestic traumas which have involved two car accidents, a slipped disc, (yet another) burglary and surgery to both of the family cats! As a result, I don't think it would have been completed at all without the friendship and support of Jane and Mike Curel, Julia Fowler and Pauline Wallace. Finally, special thanks go to my son, Haydn, for acting as computer support technician, the book's trial reader and my stress counsellor – and fetching the take-aways too. For nagging me to get the book done and for the enduring ability to make me laugh when I need to most – thanks, son.

Dee Cook
May 1997

Dee Cook is Associate Dean at the School of Humanities and Social Sciences, University of Wolverhampton.

FOREWORD

One of the many legacies of the market-driven forces that have dominated the 1980s and '90s is that quality and success in life has become measured almost entirely by economic indicators.

The result of this has been a ready and glib association between a lack of means and a lack of moral value or fibre, as if those who are well endowed imbue our society with a sense of justice and high standards. The regular and recent disclosures of the profits, earnings increments, and bonuses of those in charge of public utilities − right through to the National Lottery − give the lie to this. Those on the borders of poverty whose lives are governed by struggle and victimisation often have a clearer view of what is right and a stronger sense of conscience.

It is, however, but a short step from 'money matters' to what has now become accepted currency within all shades of the narrow, conventional political spectrum − the vilification of the vulnerable: immigrants, lone mothers, homeless people and the unemployed. They are at once uncomfortable, inconvenient, unsightly, unnecessary − a burden subsisting within a culture of dependency.

The welfare safety net must be tightened, there must be deterrents, fast-track sanctions, lock ups and zero tolerance. Ultimately the whole process becomes one of criminalisation. Survival is determined in true Darwinian fashion by the extent to which you are able not just to stand on your own two feet but on everyone else's without losing your balance or getting caught.

It is now time for a complete re-appraisal, particularly whilst the feeling of liberation brought about by the recent election result is so widespread and poignant, and the forces which have 'something of the night' are consigned to the backbench burners.

Values governed by care, community, global concern, environment, education, integration, dignity and respect have to be put squarely at the centre of the agenda. This book is an auspicious, trenchant and well researched platform for such an exercise. It courageously confronts the assumptions and moral hazards which have predicated social policy for so long – the nuclear family, the 'underclass', the permissive society.

The book points up the inherent hypocrisy, particularly within the economic system, and highlights the effects of economic inequalities which generate a context in which crime is more likely to be committed by the rich and poor alike.

For too long there has been a pre-occupation – for bland electoral reasons – with symptoms and not with causes. The criminal justice system – whether manifest through the police, prison or statute – cannot possibly provide long-term remedies and must not be traded as such any longer. Underlying societal polarisation and alienation needs to be addressed. There can be no room for complacency nor delay.

Michael Mansfield QC

Poverty and crime: the same old story?

INTRODUCTION

Most people hold firm views about crime. Whether voiced in street, doorstep or garden conversations; whether debated in pubs or parliament, crime is a topic which generates universal interest as well as strong opinions on both its causes and its remedies. Often such opinions take for granted a link between poverty and crime. Many assume that criminals, their families and the areas in which they live are 'pathological' – that crime is something apart from the everyday experience of 'normal' society, and that it is largely bred within a family and cultural context dominated by poverty. This book seeks to unravel such assumptions and to question how we think about the relationships between crime and poverty. This chapter starts by identifying the different ways of looking at the crime-poverty link, and will go on to trace how they have developed over time.

TALK ABOUT CRIME AND POVERTY

> Social deprivation can be linked to most areas of crime, and this government must address the electorate in terms of a solution. (**Commander David Stevens**, Metropolitan Police, February 1992)

> I believe [people] ... should condemn. If they do not condemn, they may appear to approve tacitly. Tacit approval will lead to repetition, and that is what we need to avoid. I feel strongly society needs to condemn a little more and understand a little less. (Prime Minister **John Major**, 1993)

You can argue forever about the causes of crime. My approach is based on some simple principles. That children – at home and at school – must be taught the difference between right and wrong. That criminals, and no one else – must be held responsible for their actions. (**Michael Howard**, Home Secretary, October 1993)

It is disorder that leads to crime and the threat of disorder that leads to crime. As the Deputy police commissioner of New York said to me last month, it was not organised crime that worried him but disorganised crime... You cannot have everything at once... While it is crucially important to provide people with jobs and decent housing, there is still something you can do about social disorder. It is irresponsible to say otherwise. (**Jack Straw**, Shadow Home Secretary, September 1995)

We will uphold family life as the most secure means of bringing up our children. Families are the core of our society. They should teach right from wrong. They should be the first defence against anti-social behaviour. (Labour Party Leader, **Tony Blair**, April 1997)

Why do people commit crime? Come in Michael Howard: of course social deprivation plays a part. Yes, they're going to get their dole money. But these people have had their hope taken away. Combine that with the fact that public morality just doesn't exist. Putting it bluntly, if someone's got a stolen telly in their front room, no one round here gives a shit. But why should they? ... How can you expect people with no future, on the poverty line, to worry about a stolen telly when the Chairman of British Gas got his whopping pay rise and his millions in share options, while his own employees are getting the sack? (**Police constable** with 20 years' service, quoted in D Rose, *In the Name of the Law*, Jonathan Cape, 1996, pp94–5)

These quotes demonstrate a range of views on the relationships between poverty and crime. Depending on the views held, they also imply very differing policies for preventing crime and punishing offenders. For Commander Stevens, most crime can be attributed to deprivation and so the crime 'problem' will only be effectively addressed by political efforts to tackle poverty. In the view of the then Home Secretary, Michael Howard, this is a 'trendy theory'. He places the blame for crime on the fatherless family and schools which 'fail to instil discipline and respect'. As a result his solutions for crime are primarily individual, moral, educative and, above all, punitive.

The punitive and moral dimensions are also implied in the quote from Prime Minister John Major. He implicitly argues that we should not try to understand crime or excuse it, but, rather roundly condemn, and so punish, all crime, however that crime may be motivated. The role of family and morality in causing crime is also emphasised by Tony Blair. According to Blair and Jack Straw (now Prime Minister and Home Secretary respectively), lack of work, family instability and homelessness also play a significant part in causing crime and disorder. For New Labour, tackling crime means tackling these causes of crime, but not necessarily as a *first* priority – if, as Jack Straw asserts, you cannot 'do everything at once', then crime control and punishment come first on the agenda.

However, the views of the long-serving police constable offer a more complex perspective which incorporates many of the themes raised by other commentators, but in a more challenging way. He feels society needs a sense of 'public morality', but this depends on a broader framework of social justice. Without a sense of fairness and social justice, criminal justice cannot be seen to be done. He goes on to argue that society cannot blame the poor for their crimes if it offers them no hope for the future *and* tolerates gross inequalities of income and wealth. These issues, which lie at the heart of this chapter and this book, are by no means new. In familiar terms, history repeats itself. In trying to understand poverty, crime and punishment as we approach the millennium, a great deal may be learned from the past.

THE 'DISHONEST' POOR

More than a century ago, the connections between social deprivation and deviance were being explored by a variety of social commentators. The social surveys of Booth and Mayhew charted the lived experiences of the nineteenth century poor, but poverty was not a unified or a clearly defined status. Its features were not only economic: the lines which demarcated the 'dangerous' and the 'dishonest poor' (from the respectable, working poor) were often **moral**. The former were often seen as a 'race apart'. They were not only distinguished by their economic dependency, but also by the degrading lifestyle which was believed to accompany this dependency.

The dangerous classes took such unrespectability to the ultimate end – criminality.[1]

The theme of morality is also evident in notions of the *deserving* and the **undeserving** poor. These distinctions were legacies of the 1834 Poor Law, whose architects believed that 'every penny bestowed' on the poor was a 'bounty on indolence and vice'. Poor relief for the able-bodied undeserving poor was regarded an incentive to idleness. And so, for many nineteenth century social commentators the 'real' social problem was not poverty itself, but the status of **pauperism**. Pauperism was 'poverty's visible form ... largely an act of will. It was freely chosen and was therefore sinful.'[2] The term 'pauper' was reserved for recipients of poor relief who were seen as languishing at the expense of the over-burdened ratepayer.

Almost a century and a half later, the language of the Poor Law was still evident in Conservative MP Rhodes Boyson's view that the cosseting welfare state weakened 'the moral fibre of our people', making them like 'broiler hens'. In a collection of essays, aptly entitled *Down With the Poor*, he continued,

> No one cares, no one bothers – why should they when the state spends all its energies taking money from the energetic, successful and thrifty to give to the idle, the failures and the feckless?[3]

It is significant that, holding views such as these, Boyson went on to play a significant part in the social security reforms of the mid 1980s as a junior minister.

By the 1980s the vocabularies of economy, morality and pathology were fused around a new, composite image of the **benefit culture**. The poor were seen as rational, economic men and women, who were responding logically to financial incentives: if living on welfare benefits offered a higher weekly income than (often low paid or casual) work, then why work? If the option of *not* working had a financial 'pay off', then idleness was inevitable. In turn, the negative moral effects of the benefit culture made it likely that idleness would be followed by 'vice'. It was, therefore, essential to put in place disincentives to claiming welfare.

Incentive was the watchword of the supply-side 1980s economics of Thatcherism in Britain and the Reagan administration in the USA. But they saw financial incentives operating very differently on the rich and on the poor. According to their arguments, if the rich were not working and investing it was because they were *not receiving enough* financial incentives to do so. It was therefore essential to provide them with added incentives (for example, through cuts in income tax and tax free investment schemes). But if the poor were not working, it was because they were *receiving too much* money from the state and lacked the incentive to work. And so, they argued, the poor needed financial **disincentives** to claiming benefits, to spur them on to greater effort.

The social policies which flowed from these views, both in the USA and Britain, have invariably meant (and still mean in the 1990s) tax cuts for the rich, and increasing stringency in welfare benefits for the poor (see Chapters 5 and 7). But such policies are two sides of the same political coin. For the New Right to effectively promote the values of the **enterprise culture** in Thatcher's Britain, they had to simultaneously denounce the evils of the dependency culture: in other words, 'for success to glisten seductively at the winners, the failure of poverty must display its burden of guilt and shame.'[4]

CRIME, MORALITY AND THE 'UNDERCLASS'

Parallel developments in the USA during the 1980s centred on precisely the same issues of morality, dependency and incentives, but this was expressed in terms of the perils of the **underclass**. The concept of an underclass, like the Thatcherite assault on the welfare state, drew heavily on the work of nineteenth century British theorists. As Himmelfarb, in a tellingly-entitled work, *The De-Moralization of Society*, noted:

> One does not need to have had a Victorian grandmother, as did Margaret Thatcher, to be reminded of 'Victorian values'. One does not even need to be English.[5]

Quite so, as the American guru of the underclass theory, Charles Murray, demonstrates when he speaks of his childhood in Iowa in these terms:

> There were two kinds of poor people. One class of people was never even called 'poor'. I came to understand that they simply lived on low incomes, as my own parents had done when they were young. There was another set of people, just a handful of them. These poor people didn't just lack money. They were defined by their behaviour. Their homes were littered and unkempt. The men in the family were

unable to hold a job for more than a few weeks at a time. Drunkenness was common. The children grew up ill-schooled and ill-behaved and contributed a disproportionate share of the local juvenile delinquents. To Henry Mayhew ... they were the 'dishonest poor'.[6]

One hundred and forty years on, this interpretation of Mayhew remains fundamental to the concepts of both dependency culture and underclass. But these are not just abstract concepts – they give rise to policies which have very real effects. Crucially, they are widely echoed in political and judicial pronouncements about poverty, welfare and crime. For example, in 1989 the then Secretary of State for Social Security, John Moore, spoke of the evils of the 'benefit culture' in strikingly similar terms to his nineteenth century counterparts. Moore denied the very existence of poverty in a land, characterised by 'affluence beyond the wildest dreams' of the Victorians, where

> even the poorest fifth of families spend nearly a tenth of their income on alcohol and tobacco.[7]

It is significant that identical vocabularies – emphasising the evils of alcohol and individual fecklessness – can still be found in the justifications used by sentencers when punishing the poor. In observations of DSS fraud cases passing through one Midlands magistrates' court (conducted in 1991), one chairman of the bench consistently asked all social security defendants who passed before him whether they smoked (and, if so, 'how many a day?') and if they drank (if so, 'how many pints?'). He went on to ask one young man, who had just pleaded guilty to failing to declare earnings while claiming benefit, 'What is the price of a pint of beer?'

He received the confident response, 'About £1.35, Sir.'

The defendant was then asked if he knew the price of a pint of milk, to which he replied, 'No'. The Chairman commented that the young man was 'drinking the wrong thing', and could clearly afford the £200 fine which was then imposed.[8] This young man was (on the basis of this brief exchange about his consumer knowledge and drinking habits) judged to be (morally) irresponsible and incapable of adequately managing his limited resources. It is therefore deeply ironic that the magistrate imposed a fine, which could only worsen the offender's financial difficulties. Nonetheless, this case demonstrates how (magistrates') views on the links between crime and poverty can shape criminal justice practice.

Although the language and the categorising of the 'dangerous' and 'dishonest poor' may at first appear dated, these historical concepts still shape the ways in which we think and speak about today's 'undeserving' poor. They inform our understanding of both the general effects of welfare (in terms of the dependency culture) and the particular dishonesty of the poor (in terms of social security fraud). As Chapter 6 will go on to argue, the contemporary image of the **scrounger** reflects historical notions of the undeserving and dishonest poor, and in so doing performs similar functions of social division and criminalisation.

POVERTY, DE-MORALISATION AND BLAME

Historically, the idea that the poor were a 'race apart' has provided an important metaphor through which crime could be understood. Nineteenth century language describing the children of the dishonest poor was informed by deeper notions of Britishness and 'civilisation'. References to 'street Arabs' and 'savages' and the Irish derivation of the term 'hooligan' reflect nineteenth century imperialist and (what would now be termed racist) assumptions about crime in a 'civilised' society.[9]

Poverty was believed to generate an 'uncivil' cultural background in which crime would flourish, particularly among immigrant groups and the young. Once again, there are important historical continuities in the ways in which juvenile crime is still, in the late 1990s, seen as the product of poverty, individual wickedness and a 'race' or culture characterised by recklessness and short-termism (see Chapter 7).

But the emergence of a new (Victorian) liberalism signalled a shift in the way in which the actions of the individual 'pauper' were conceived. Instead of being seen as blameworthy, responsible individuals (who were at times capable of wilful, irresponsible acts), they were increasingly seen as shaped by dire personal and social circumstances beyond their control – as essentially inadequate and not to blame. In other words, they may be weak, but were not wholly wicked, because, it was argued, deviants were not 'born' but 'made'.

> As a rule a man [sic] is shaped by the surroundings in which he has been born and is obliged to live. If these surroundings are all calculated to injure him and to degrade him he will sooner or later degenerate and become a pauper, a lunatic or a criminal, or, as not

infrequently happens, a combination of all. (Revd W D Morrison, 1896)

The level at which human behaviour was explained therefore shifted from the **individual** to the **social**, and with it shifted the point at which policy intervention should take place. If pauperism, dishonesty and lunacy were seen to be generated by 'surroundings', then those surroundings would have to be the focus of change. The notion of an individual whose behaviour was determined by wickedness and 'vice' was now counter-balanced by a stress on the powerful influence of poverty and deprivation.

Explanations for crime in the 1990s are still often polarised between those which stress individual blame and those which stress the socio-economic roots of crime (as the quotations which opened this chapter demonstrate). But in the nineteenth century, as now, perspectives like these saw the link between poverty and crime as one of simple **cause and effect**. As such, they did not question that there *was* a causal link between pauperism and crime. Instead, the key question was one of how (social) scientists could better understand the 'laws' which were at work in producing crime among the poor, in order to break the chains of causation. One of these 'chains' was the thread of morality.

RE-MORALISATION AND THE 'NEW RABBLE'

The Victorian impetus to 're-moralise' the poor initially focused on the role of religion, charity and education (with a strongly 'moral' tone). More than a century later, the strength of this impetus should not be underestimated. Over the last 15 years, calls for a return to 'Victorian values' (under Thatcher), 'back to basics' (under Major) and the stress on 'family values' under New Labour have all demonstrated the enduring political appeal of re-moralisation as a solution to a variety of social ills: these ills range from crime and poor academic standards in schools (blamed on bad parenting and even worse teaching by the children of the 'permissive sixties') to urban blight (blamed on a lack of responsibility and civic values).

Within such explanations for social problems, crime and illegitimacy are highest on the re-moraliser's hit list. But in both cases their remedy involves **blaming the victim** and so offers only a pseudo-solution (attacking the outward 'symptoms' of social ills may well just deflect attention from the root causes). In 1992 the Conservative Home Office Minister, John Patten, emphasised the role of morality when asserting that 'there are no excuses for lawlessness and hooliganism.' This view was challenged by Labour Leader Tony Blair, in a 'famous soundbite, declaring his aim to be "tough on crime, tough on the causes of crime".'[10] But, since 1992, Tony Blair has begun a retreat to the safer territory of moral crusade as the main thrust of New Labour's law and order policy.

When examining how we think about crime and poverty the theme of morality is therefore important for two fundamental reasons:

- immorality is seen as a central feature of the underclass or dependency culture, within which, it is argued, most crime is committed (but, see Chapter 3 for an alternative view);
- if it is a lack of morality which produces crime, then re-moralisation offers a remedy for crime and lawlessness.

This re-moralisation has focused on both the family and the welfare state. As we have already seen, notions of the negative effects of the benefit culture and of the perils of the underclass both stress that the post-war welfare state has **de-moralised** society. Not only has the welfare state turned benefit recipients into 'broiler hens', but claiming benefit is in itself presented as a '*moral* hazard':

> A consequence of the widespread dependence on means-tested benefits is that the young in particular feel no stigma when they claim benefit. We are producing a race which will regard dependence on the taxpayer as a normal state of affairs. Already the young claim social security without hesitation as a matter of right.[11]

According to such views it is amoral to *not* feel stigmatised by claiming benefit (a view reminiscent of the deterrent principles of the 1834 Poor Law). Once again the young are prime targets, as they constitute the able-bodied, **undeserving poor**. Parker's view totally undercuts the notion of a citizen's *right* to welfare and does not acknowledge the obvious point that dependence on the taxpayer is bound to be a 'normal state of affairs' if you cannot obtain regular paid work!

One corollary of this argument about dependency is that unemployment effectively prevents young men from taking on the personal and financial responsibilities which are appropriate to their age and status. If unemployment denies young men (sic) their financial independence, then it is tantamount to a denial of their full adulthood. The logic of this argument means that if society wants young people (and young men in particular) to 'grow up', gain a sense of responsibility, and keep out of trouble, we need to give them the opportunity to work.

But, for some authors, it is not lack of work that is the key problem for young men – it is lack of **family** responsibilities.[12] The provision of welfare benefits, it is argued, undermines the establishment and the continuance of 'traditional' gender roles and **traditional family values**. For young men, the 'sexual constitution of welfare ... tells them money is a bequest for women rather than the earnings of men' and, as a result, men find their basic role of provider undermined – they are 'cuckolded by the compassionate state'.[13] According to such views, it is the erosion of 'traditional' masculinity, and not poverty itself, that has led to unprecedented increases in crime among young men.

> If we are looking for something that has profoundly changed for young males in the twenty or thirty years during which many of them have gone on the rampage, it is not increasing poverty. We have become richer ... It is not high unemployment. The trend in crime rate has been upward through periods of low unemployment. It is the social definition of what it is to be a man.[14]

If we are to take this argument at face value, it suggests that law and (social) order depends on young men being prevented from engaging in criminal 'rampage' by the bonds of the traditional male-bread-winner/female-dependant relationship. This relationship is cemented by the institution of **marriage** which, according to Charles Murray, is 'indispensable' for the 'liberal society'. He considers a society's marriage rate as an index of social order and calls upon the state to 'stop penalising marriage'. But Murray also calls for the penalisation of 'illegitimate births', notably those which occur among the 'new rabble':

> Illegitimacy in the lower classes will continue to rise and, inevitably, life in lower class communities will continue to degenerate – more crime, more widespread drug and alcohol addiction, fewer marriages, more drop-out from work, more homelessness, more child neglect, fewer young people pulling themselves out of the slums, more young people tumbling in.[15]

For 'new rabble' we could easily read 'new dishonest poor' as, once again, history repeats itself. Moreover, Murray's words appear to echo those (20 years earlier) of the Secretary of State for Social Services, Sir Keith Joseph, whose call for 'the re-moralisation of public life' was uncomfortably dressed in the language of eugenics.

> The balance of our population, our human stock is threatened ... a high and rising proportion of children are being born to mothers least fitted to bring children into the world. Many of these girls [from social classes 4 and 5] are unmarried, many are deserted or divorced or soon will be ... They are producing problem children, the future unmarried mothers, delinquents, denizens of our borstals, sub-normal educational establishments, prisons, hostels for drifters.
> (Sir Keith Joseph, 19 October 1974)

Again, the poor are portrayed as a 'race apart', and they are responsible for breeding (quite literally) a plethora of social problems. At the forefront of these problems is crime. Crime is regarded as an integral feature of the life of the poor: it is one which they are seen to physically reproduce, from one generation to the next, primarily through the medium of single parent families. For example, when describing the three **symptoms** of the underclass, Murray cites 'crime, illegitimacy and economic inactivity among working age men'.[16] But these three components of de-moralisation are, at the same time, seen as the *causes* of crime itself:

- **'rampaging' young men** (whose manliness has been undermined by the sexual constitution of welfare);
- **'least fitted' young women** (ie, those from socio-economic classes 4–5) bearing children out of wedlock;
- **the moral hazard of the benefit culture** (for the able-bodied, 'undeserving' poor).

In this circular argument the *causes* of crime are conflated with the *features* of those individuals and groups who have (already) been defined as crime-prone. In such simplistic theories, the causal relationship between crime and poverty is *assumed* but is not demonstrated or logically argued through.

CRIME AND 'PROBLEM FAMILIES'

The notion that crime 'runs in the family' is a simple and popular theme which has influenced the ways in which the links between crime and poverty have been conceptualised. At a basic level, this theme has two versions:

- first, that criminal tendencies are inherited;
- secondly, that delinquency is the product of family environment.

According to the first version, historical analyses of pauperism and crime supposedly revealed the existence of criminal 'bloodlines'.[17] According to the second, crime was the product of the 'under the roof culture' of dysfunctional families.[18] The implications of both views are that the poor 'breed crime', and that they generate a family-based culture within which crime flourishes.

Although it may be tempting to argue that notions of crime as 'in the blood' are out of date, we should be wary of such optimism. After all, it is only 20 years since the influential Sir Keith Joseph spoke of the breeding habits of mothers from the lower socio-economic groups. And, in the 1990s, recent statements by right-wing politicians, such as John Redwood, have fuelled a similar 'moral panic' over lone mothers (discussed in more depth in Chapter 7). Contemporary accounts of the 'born' and the 'made' criminal are also encompassed in the overarching theme of the 'problem family'.

For some commentators the **problem family** label can be regarded, historically, as a social product, generated by emerging professions with ambitions to play a part in the criminal justice and penal systems by offering their varied insights on family pathology. According to such views the postwar emergence of psychiatry, psychoanalysis, sociology and social work all intersected on the problem family.[19] The family was the target of their support, but it was also the target of their policing interventions.

According to Donzelot,[20] this was part of a broader impetus to secure social order and integration by policing the poor – and policing the poor was, in part, accomplished by defining and regulating the poor's 'problem families'. This involved those key professionals in a three stage process:

- identifying and notifying 'problem' children and families;
- inquiring and assessing the problem;
- taking charge and giving 'tutelage' to control the problem.

For the poor family caught up in this process there may be a 'Catch 22' effect, which serves to justify the 'problem' labels which had been applied to them in the first place. The way in which families are processed by professional agencies can, it is argued, close the rhetorical circle which links poverty, problem family and crime. The following hypothetical example demonstrates this process.

> A large working class family lives in a modern but cramped apartment. The mother sends the older children outside so as to be able to attend to the younger ones. She is what is called an 'over-burdened' mother. The father, when he comes home from work, demands quiet and turns on the television or reads his newspaper instead of devoting himself to educative talks with the children. He is what is called an 'inaccessible' father. Consequently, life in the street forms a large part of the children's framework of existence, with all this implies in the way of 'bad company' and exposure to police authority. So, depending on whether the parents prepare for the possibility of the police arresting their children by alerting a social worker, or cover for them, reckoning that if the children hang out in the street it is nothing serious, nor are they to blame, the parents will be classified as either 'overly protective' or 'rejecting'.[21]

There is no clear dividing line between the **problem family** and what can be termed the 'criminogenic' or **crime-prone family**. They exist at different points of a **social problem – crime** continuum in which the boundaries (of what is a 'social' and what is a 'crime' problem) are very blurred. But all along this continuum there is a presumption that a family's 'chronic problems' *cause* criminal behaviour. The work of West, who conducted a series of longitudinal studies of delinquency between 1969 and 1982, exemplifies this view:

> The typical criminogenic family is beset by chronic problems … parents who let their children spend most of their leisure time away from the family, fathers who never took part in their son's leisure activities and mothers whose expectations of their son's future career were low in comparison with his educational achievement, were all more likely than others to have sons becoming delinquent.[22]

But perspectives on the links between crime and poor families are not just of 'academic' interest for two reasons: first, because they form part of a long and complex legacy of ideas which shape the way we *all* think about crime. Secondly, views such as these go on to have very real effects because they are regularly reproduced in *practice* by criminal justice professionals.[23] Chapter 4 will go on to examine, in more detail, how the sentencing process reflects and reproduces the image of the criminogenic family.

CRIME AND LOCALITY: 'PROBLEM' AREAS

The idea of the **criminal area** has a long history and its legacy can be traced in contemporary descriptions and accounts of crime in poorer localities. Contemporary exposés of inner city deprivation (and depravity) have many of the hallmarks of Mayhew's description of the nineteenth century's criminal areas, the 'rookeries': squalid housing, overcrowding, gambling, vice (notably prostitution), drunkenness, petty theft and hardened criminals, together with a powerful sense of 'danger'. But the language associated with the rookeries has, in the late twentieth century, been modified by recent political events: foremost amongst such events have been the 'riots' which occurred in several British cities in 1981, 1985 and 1991. One crucial dimension of the change in how we conceptualise the criminal areas has been the **racialisation** of the 'urban crisis'.

Although very aware of the complexities involved in understanding the concepts of both 'race' and the 'city', Michael Keith describes the ways in which 'race' can be 'used systematically to conjure up the urban crisis'. In general terms, 'Blackness ... has come to play a cautionary role' which may be likened to the nineteenth century fears of the crowd and the dangerous classes.[24]

A prime example of this tendency is evident in a speech made by the Metropolitan Police Commissioner, Sir Kenneth Newman, in the wake of the 1981 inner city 'riots', where he coined the term 'symbolic location' to describe what in essence were the (racialised) features of 'problem' areas.

> Throughout London there are locations where unemployed youth – often black youths – congregate; where the sale and purchase of drugs, the exchange of stolen property and illegal drinking and gaming is not uncommon. The youths regard these locations as their territory. Police are viewed as intruders, the symbol of authority – largely white authority – in a society that is responsible for all their grievances about unemployment, prejudice and discrimination. They equate closely with criminal 'rookeries' of Dickensian London ... If allowed to continue, locations with these characteristics assume symbolic importance and negative symbolism of the inability of the police to maintain order. Their existence encourages law-breaking elsewhere, affects public perceptions of police effectiveness, heightens fear of crime and reinforces a phenomenon of urban decay.[25]

The fact that the leading police chief in the country held such views is particularly significant and his views about the territoriality of Black* youth proved powerful. Moreover, the logic of this argument, that there should be no 'no-go areas' for the English police, was highly influential. Since 1983, riot training has become a compulsory element in all police force training, and the targeting of potentially 'symbolic locations' has become an integral part of policing strategy and the deployment of police resources.

Popular and political fears about 'no-go' areas in British cities spread throughout the 1980s, although policy solutions did not focus on the structural problems of poverty, unemployment and racism (identified in the Scarman Report) which many saw at the root of unrest. Instead, a good deal of policy effort was directed at improving the architectural environment within which those problems were lived and realised. For instance, in response to the Toxteth riots, the Secretary of State for the Environment, Michael Heseltine, announced that Liverpool was to host a Garden Festival. Similarly, Margaret Thatcher, in a post-election photo-call on a derelict urban site, confirmed her intention to attack the outward manifestations of urban decline, but failed to acknowledge or address its root causes (see discussion of widening social and economic inequalities in Chapter 2).

As part of the policy thrust towards environmental solutions, the concept of **defensible space** was resurrected to both explain and to offer practical solutions in the wake of what was seen as a law and order crisis in British inner cities. The explanations offered for this crisis were contradictory. On the one hand, the riots were represented as 'race riots' while, on the other, they were seen as the product of unsafe and insecure places which were, in terms of design, havens for the criminal. In particular, the Broadwater Farm estate, the location of one notorious 'riot' (or 'uprising' or 'disturbance', depending on your perspective) in 1985, seemed to support the 'design causes crime' hypothesis.

But by the 1990s, it became apparent that both explanations were deeply flawed. Neither 'race' nor a lack of defensible space could explain the events of 1991, when riots erupted in predominantly white and/or 'suburban' localities such as Blackbird Leys, Oxford and

*Note: The term 'Black' is used to describe all those non-white minority ethnic groups who experience discrimination. This usage in no way implies that all minority ethnic groups share the same experiences or sense of identity: when referring to such differences or to literature which uses alternative categories, distinctions will be made.

Scotswood, Tyneside – these areas possessed defensible spaces and so did not 'fit' the profile.[26] It is important to recognise that estate design represents only one feature of any explanation for social disorder and crime. As Campbell has pointed out, the problem of the architecture and the residents became inseparable.

> The theory of the underclass entered the vernacular together with the image of the *estate*. The two became synonymous in Britain.[27]

She goes on to summarise how the **spatialisation** of crime had changed by the nineties.

> The collective gaze was directed at localities rather than, for example, the grandiose corporate frauds which vexed, and ultimately exhausted, the judicial system … the 'symbolic locations' shifted from … the inner city … to the edge of the city … These were places that were part of a mass landscape in Britain, *estates* were everywhere. But in the Nineties, estates came to mean crime.[28]

Crime was now conceived as a 'mass' phenomenon, not confined to the inner city, but everywhere and anywhere. (But, as will be discussed in Chapter 3, policing effort was directed to crime in the streets not the business suites.) The estate metaphor did not only incorporate the notion of unpopular and run-down *areas* as crime prone, but focused on their 'least eligible' inhabitants, too.

> Everyone with a young family and a little bit of intelligence wants to move off … We're getting the waifs and strays (Resident quoted in *Swimming Against the Tide*, 1995).[29]

Once again, the notion of an underclass is a recurring image, one which may have a direct effect on the everyday lives of estate residents:

> I don't tell people where I live. (Resident)

> I visited some local employers and found that they employed no-one from the estate because the youth on the estate were thought to be trouble. (Local Estate Manager)

Both of these quotations are taken from a recent analysis of patterns of polarisation on 20 'unpopular estates' between 1980 and 1995: the study reveals a striking concentration of individual and social problems in these hardest-to-let estates (see summary in Figure 1.1).

Taken together, these problems create a spiral of social decline which is extremely hard to break. It is not surprising that the research comes to the conclusion that crime is not just a product of estate design, but the product of more complex social factors (see Chapter 2 for further discussion of social disorganisation, crime, social exclusion and the 'sink estate').

As Figure 1.1 demonstrates, the chaotic conditions of these estates are produced by a combination of factors, including the social composition of residents, housing policy, lettings systems and local estate management.[30] Although case studies show that some of these problems can be tackled, this requires both resources and strong political will.

Figure 1.1: **Outline of patterns of social decline on estates**

Poor physical and social conditions

Applicants with choice are deterred

Low social status of estate

Estates become harder to let

High turnover and vacancies

More vulnerable groups get housed

More difficulty in managing estates

More damage and disrepair

More unpopular – more exit

Lack of social cohesion

Breakdown in social controls

Difficulty in maintaining management control

Poorer conditions

Other services adversely affected

Chaotic conditions

Source: A Power and R Tunstall, *Swimming Against the Tide: polarisation or progress on 20 unpopular council estates, 1980-1995*, Joseph Rowntree Foundation, 1995.

SUMMARY

This chapter started by looking at how key politicians and police officers saw the relationship between poverty and crime. Their views can be seen to reflect two very different positions on crime and the extent to which the individual is responsible for it:

1 Crime is linked with social deprivation, and so the individual is not entirely to blame.
2 Crime is a matter of 'right and wrong', and individuals must be held responsible for their actions.

These positions, in turn, imply very different policy solutions:

1 Politicians must tackle poverty and reduce social inequality to give individuals a sense of social (as well as criminal) justice.
2 Society should not try to understand or excuse crime, but should condemn, deter and punish it more effectively.

Of course, not all views on crime, poverty and punishment are so neatly divided. But these positions form the two end points of the spectrum.

We have seen that such views are by no means new. The debate over the individual versus the social causes of (and solutions for) crime has a long history. In trying to engage with this debate in the 1990s, we are bound to tap into the rich reservoir of past images and assumptions. In a brief outline of some of the key images and assumptions of the nineteenth century, I have argued that our views about poverty, crime and punishment have been shaped by a variety of historical themes, including:

- distinctions between the **respectable, dishonest and dangerous poor**;
- distinctions between the **deserving and the undeserving poor**;
- the poor as a **race apart**;
- the moral evils of **welfare dependency**;
- the crime-prone character of the **benefit culture and the underclass**;
- the **decline of the 'traditional family'** as a cause of crime;
- crime as the product of **family culture or pathology**;
- **symbolic locations** as a context for crime;
- the **racialisation** of crime and the urban crisis; *and*
- the **spatialisation** of crime, from the 'rookery' to the 'sink estate'.

NOTES

1. G Himmelfarb, *The Idea of Poverty: England in the Early Industrial Age*, Faber and Faber, 1984.
2. G Stedman Jones, 'The threat of outcast London' in M Fitzgerald, G McLennan and J Pawson (eds), *Crime and Society*, RKP, 1981, p177.
3 R Boyson, *Down With the Poor*, Churchill Press, 1971, p5.

4   P Golding and S Middleton, *Images of Welfare*, Martin Robertson, 1982, p244.

5   G Himmelfarb, *The De-Moralization of Society: from Victorian virtues to modern values*, IEA Health and Welfare Unit, Choice in Welfare Series No 22, 1995, p221.

6   C Murray, *The Emerging British Underclass*, IEA, 1990, p1.

7   *Guardian*, 12 May 1989.

8   D Cook, 'Social Disadvantage and Offending', unpublished paper to NAPO Bail Hostels Conference, UMIST, September 1991, p5.

9   G Pearson, *Hooligan: a history of respectable fears*, Macmillan, 1983; R Dallos and E McLaughlin (eds), *Social Problems and the Family*, Sage, 1993.

10   D Rose, *In the Name of the Law*, Jonathan Cape, 1996, p93.

11   H Parker, *The Moral Hazards of Social Benefits*, Research Monograph, IEA, 1982.

12   N Dennis and G Erdos, *Families Without Fatherhood*, IEA Health and Welfare Unit, Choice in Welfare No 12, 1995.

13   G Gilder, quoted in M Loney, *The Politics of Greed*, Pluto Press, 1986, p31.

14   N Dennis, *Rising Crime and the Dismembered Family*, IEA Health and Welfare Unit, Choice in Welfare Series No 18, 1993, p9.

15   C Murray, *Underclass: the crisis deepens*, IEA Health and Welfare Unit, Choice in Welfare No 20, 1994, p18.

16   *Ibid*, p2.

17   R J Sapsford, 'Individual deviance: the search for the criminal personality' in Fitzgerald *et al* (eds), *see* note 2.

18   R Dallos, 'Moral development and the family: the genesis of crime' in Fitzgerald *et al* (eds), *see* note 2.

19   B Hudson, *Justice Through Punishment*, Macmillan, 1987.

20   J Donzelot, *The Policing of Families*, Hutchinson, 1980.

21   *Ibid*, p158.

22   D West, *Delinquency: its roots, careers and prospects*, Heinemann Educational, 1982, pp56-7.

23   S Brown, *Magistrates at Work*, Open University Press, 1990.

24   M Keith and M Cross, 'Racism and the post-modern city' in M Keith and M Cross (eds), *Racism, the City and the State*, Routledge, 1993, p10.

25   Sir Kenneth Newman, quoted in P Gilroy and J Sim, 'Law and order and the state of the Left', in *Capital and Class*, No 25, 1985.

26   B Campbell, *Goliath*, Methuen, 1993.

27   *Ibid*, p314.

28   *Ibid*, p317.

29   A Power and R Tunstall, *Swimming Against the Tide: polarisation and progress on 20 unpopular council estates, 1980–1995*, Joseph Rowntree Foundation, 1995, p15.

30   *Ibid*, p58.

Contemporary patterns of poverty and inequality are the inevitable legacy of post-1979 social and fiscal policies.

Credit: Ulrike Preuss/Format

2 Poverty, inequality and crime

INTRODUCTION

> Policy makers should be concerned with the way in which the living standards of a substantial minority of the population have lagged behind since the late 1970s. Not only is this a problem for those directly affected, it also damages the social fabric and so affects us all ... Regardless of any moral arguments or feelings of altruism, everyone shares an interest in the cohesiveness of society. As the gaps between rich and poor grow, the problems of the marginalised groups which are being left behind rebound on the more comfortable majority. (Joseph Rowntree Foundation, *Inquiry into Income and Wealth*, Vol 1, 1995, p8)

The Joseph Rowntree Foundation's *Inquiry into Income and Wealth*[1] drew on original research and a wide range of existing studies and government statistics in its comprehensive mapping of patterns of income and wealth distribution in Britain in the 1990s. The conclusions were alarming: they exploded the myth that British society was becoming more equal. The post-war welfare state had not effectively performed a redistributive role – taking from the rich and giving to the poor. The evidence indicated that the reverse was true: since the 1970s, the rich were getting richer and the poor were getting poorer still.

This chapter will, first, explore changing patterns of poverty and wealth over the past two decades; secondly, assess the implications of these patterns for the everyday lives of both the 'marginalised' and the 'comfortable majority'; thirdly, critically assess the popular view that poverty and unemployment **cause** crime.

POVERTY – WHAT POVERTY?

By any absolute standard there is very little poverty in Britain today. There are those who, like the old and the disabled, widows and some one parent families, have special needs. There are other cases of poverty of a kind which no society can entirely eliminate because they result from, say, gross mismanagement, alcoholism or some unforeseen disaster. (Sir Keith Joseph, 1979)[2]

Chapter 1 has examined how the categories of deserving and undeserving poor have shaped popular mythologies about crime and poverty. This quotation illustrates the influence of such categories on social policy-makers. In effectively declaring 'the end of poverty', Sir Keith Joseph's case rested on two axioms:

- a definition of poverty which is **absolute**, not relative;
- a distinction between those who are **responsible** for their own poverty and those who are blameless.

In addition to denying the existence of poverty, this extract also indicates the view that the relief of poverty is not the job of the State, except in exceptional, defined and deserving cases. But, at the same time, Peter Townsend produced an alternative definition, which called for a very different level of intervention:

Individuals, families and groups in the population can be said to be in poverty when they lack the resources to obtain the type of diet, participate in the activities and have the living conditions and amenities which are customary, or at least widely encouraged, or approved, in the societies to which they belong. They are, in effect, excluded from ordinary living patterns, customs and activities.[3]

Central to this definition is the concept of poverty as **relative**. Such definitions, and their focus on social not individual pathology, are implicit in the work of what has been termed 'the poverty lobby'. But these perspectives remain vigorously contested: many right-wing opponents continue to see the issue of poverty as, in the words of Margaret Thatcher, a problem of 'bourgeois guilt'. For instance, in *Taking the Measure of Poverty*, Pryke argues that as 'mass poverty does not exist, there is no call for the feelings of guilt which are generated by its supposed existence'.[4]

But clearly poverty cannot be reduced to a problem of guilt and intellectual angst: it is a problem which has material and psychological effects on those individuals and groups who experience it. (The reality of the problem of poverty is clear from its impact on individual health – research by the Kings Fund published in 1995 concluded that 42,000 lives a year could be saved in Britain if the health of the poorest citizens matched the level of the richest.[5]) Moreover, contemporary patterns of poverty and inequality can be regarded as the inevitable legacy of post-1979 social and fiscal policies.

THE LEGACY OF THATCHERISM

A decade ago CPAG's publication, *The Growing Divide: a social audit 1979-87*,[6] persuasively argued that the growth of poverty and inequality during the first eight years of Thatcherism were not accidental, but an inevitable outcome of government policies because, in the words of a former Minister for Social Security,

> If you believe economic salvation can only be achieved by rewarding success and the national income is not increasing, then you have no alternative but to make the unsuccessful poorer. (Reg Prentice, 1979)[7]

Over the last decade this **strategy of inequality** has been pursued through a variety of mechanisms, but most notably through successive changes in taxation which have included:

- reductions in the higher rate of income tax for the rich (from 60 per cent to 40 per cent);
- higher thresholds for inheritance tax for the rich;
- a policy spotlight on reducing the basic rate of income tax (of no benefit to the poorest and non-taxpaying groups);
- a shift from direct to indirect taxation, particularly through VAT (penalising the poor);
- an increase in the overall burden of taxation on (middle and) lower income groups;
- the council tax (disenfranchising and impoverishing many poorer and multi-occupied households).

An important watershed in tax and social security policy was 1988: in this year, Nigel Lawson's tax give-away Budget marked a deliberate acceleration in the growing trend towards inequality. According to Margaret Thatcher, 'Nigel's Budget was the obituary for the doctrine of high taxation ... It was the epitaph for socialism.'

In reducing the highest rate of income tax from 60 per cent to 40 per cent, Lawson gave a total of £2 billion in tax cuts to the top 5 per cent of wage earners, while the lowest 30 per cent received virtually nothing. This Budget embodied the New Right vision of how fiscal incentives operated in the enterprise culture, but the fallacy of this vision is evident in the reaction of one 'Tory entrepreneur' to yet more cuts in his income tax.

> I think Nigel's taking the piss now ... I don't think anyone will work any harder. I certainly won't work any harder, I'll just spend more ... People will have three skiing holidays instead of one.[8]

Lawson had argued that *everyone* would benefit from his Budget tax cuts. His 'trickledown' theory argued that the economic growth unleashed by the enterprise culture (now, unfettered by the disincentive effects of high taxes) would eventually cascade down to poorer groups. But all empirical evidence points to the contrary.[9]

Meanwhile, the 1988 Social Security Reforms demonstrated the other side of the incentives coin: for example, the abolition of exceptional needs payments and concomitant establishment of the finite social fund (with repayable loans) were to 'encourage claimants to take more responsibility for their own spending', while the principles of less eligibility were evident in the reforms' emphases on work testing and the principles of 'targeting' and 'desert'.[10] In this way, changes in social security and taxation policy intensified inequality through tax cuts for the rich and benefit cuts for the poor.

By 1991, and the demise of Margaret Thatcher, 52 per cent of the tax cuts implemented by her governments since 1979 had gone to the top 10 per cent of income earners.[11] At the same time, the real value of most social security benefits had fallen markedly, accentuated by the fact that they were pegged to the price index (RPI) rather than to earnings, which rose much more steeply. And so, rather than mitigating its worst effects, the social security system has contributed to an *increase* in social inequality since the early 1980s.

> In contrast to the rest of the post-war period, the incomes of the poorest groups in 1991/92 were no higher than those of the equivalent groups 12–13 years earlier. Measured after allowing for housing costs, the incomes of the poorest tenth in 1991/92 were 17 per cent lower in real terms than those of the equivalent group in 1979.[12]

Another striking feature of contemporary patterns of economic inequality is the changed **shape** of income distribution. This is a consequence of several factors, including:[13]

- more people dependent on state benefits (with almost 10 million people depending on income support in 1995);
- a growing gap between households with and those without work – **work rich and work poor** households;
- relatively lower levels of social security benefits (pegged to RPI, not earnings);
- increasing inequality *within* the 'in work' group, and the deepening problem of low pay;*
- rising female labour which has meant more (low paid) two-earner households (but there are more *non-earner* households too!);
- in non-earner households, a decline in the chances of (either partner) getting back to work;
- discretionary tax changes which have 'cancelled out' any redistributive effects of the tax/welfare system;
- a redistribution in the burden of taxation from higher to middle and lower income groups.

Other noteworthy trends in patterns of inequality arise from international comparisons: in a survey of 12 industrialised countries (1977 to 1990), the majority displayed an increase in inequality, but the **speed** of the increase was much faster in Britain than in other comparable nations. In addition, the **absolute** increase in inequality index was far higher in Britain.[15] Since 1977, the proportion of the British population with less than half of the average income – one measure of 'poverty' – has more than trebled.[16]

Distribution of wealth is even more unequal than that of income and has remained substantially unchanged over recent decades: the wealthiest 10 per cent of adults who owned 50 per cent of marketable wealth in 1976 still owned 49 per cent in 1992.[17] The much vaunted 'shareholding and property owning democracy' of the 1980s

---

* The deepening problem of low pay was undoubtedly influenced by the government's abolition of wages councils, which regulated the wages paid in specific sectors of the economy. Two years after the councils' abolition (as part of the government's policy of de-regulating the economy) research by the Low Pay Unit examined the wages offered in the former wages council sectors: it found that over a half of jobs advertised at local JobCentres were paying rates below wages council minimum rates.[14]

has, therefore, failed to make any lasting impact on the concentration of wealth holdings. Additionally, job insecurity and negative equity have taken their toll and, for the majority of British citizens, wealth ownership is an illusory concept: for instance, a 1991/92 survey showed that half of families had financial assets of less than £500, and 90 per cent less than £8,000.[18] Even the better-off elderly citizens find themselves **asset rich, but income poor**, as state pensions and 'community care' fail to deliver their promised safeguards for old age.

THE 'HAVES' AND THE 'HAVE NOTS'

Although the growth in inequality traced here *may* have slowed down since 1991, it is too early to talk of any sustained economic trends.[19] There is much evidence that the divide generated in the Thatcher years not only remains, but has become part of the social, economic and physical landscape of Britain in the late 1990s.

Two recent press items graphically illustrate the nature of this landscape and the extent of the divide between rich and poor. First, figures from Datamonitor Management Consultants indicate a dramatic rise in the numbers of millionaires in Britain from 31,000 in 1991 to 81,000 by the end of 1995.[20] Secondly, recent press coverage also reveals that the 'Mayfair millionaires' who live in the Westminster City Council area are paying less council tax than residents in Oldham, as a result of allegedly 'rigged' systems of funding Conservative councils. Consequently, the owner of a £3 million, 40-room listed building in Mayfair pays £590 tax, compared with the owner of a £41,000 terraced house in Oldham who pays £597.[21]

While the 'haves' enjoy rising living standards, the experience of the 'have nots' is characterised by the deepening crises of long-term unemployment, neighbourhood disadvantage, social exclusion and debt. A study of the experiences of 74 low income families in British inner–city areas[22] demonstrates a range of responses, many necessarily short term, to these crises. The research illustrates these responses by way of a hierarchy of options available to these families (see Figure 2.1).

The use of strategies higher up the list is limited by structural constraints: for example, those who are unemployed or have experienced long-term low pay will not have savings to draw on.

Progress lower down the list involves a narrowing of options and a progressive move towards socially unacceptable behaviour, including benefit fraud (which may be incorporated in the option of 'casual work, with income not fully disclosed' – in other words, working and not fully declaring the income to social security officials) and petty crime. However, neither of these forms of crime is an *inevitable* response to poverty, nor are they determined or *fixed* at a particular point in the hierarchy of options. For instance, benefit fraud (as argued in Chapter 5) may be regarded as a crime of poverty, but poverty alone is not a sufficient condition for its commission – not *all* claimants fiddle their benefits. At the same time, much petty crime is opportunistic (and so could theoretically occur at any level in the hierarchy) – but not *all* the urban poor commit petty crime!

Figure 2.1: **Hierarchy of options facing families with inadequate resources**

SUBJECT TO STRUCTURAL CONSTRAINTS

Find better paid full-time work

Spend 'savings'

Claim benefit

Sell non-essential possessions

Use consumer credit for regular expenditure

Delay paying bills

Take casual work (often above earnings disregard)

Cash insurance policies

Pawn valuables

Sell essential possessions

Charity

Petty crime

Begging (unacceptable)

SOCIALLY UNACCEPTABLE BEHAVIOUR

Sources: Kempson *et al*, *Hard Times*, PSI, 1994; R Walker, 'The dynamics of poverty and social exclusion' in G Room (ed), *Beyond the Threshold: the measurement and analysis of social exclusion*, 1995.

The usefulness of this analysis is, therefore, in the way it identifies a downward progression (or spiral) which may lead some individuals into choosing the option of crime. It also indicates how some families manage to 'keep their heads above water', but others 'drown'.

For the latter, their lives are characterised by multiple debt, no prospect of circumstances improving and being confronted by unacceptable options.[23]

These choices are made in contexts which are structured spatially as well as economically. As Chapter 1 argued, issues of locality are crucial to understanding the experiences of poverty, crime and criminal victimisation. The neighbourhood is, therefore, a pivotal factor in a 'complex web of inter-relationships' which also includes 'demographic, social, cultural and lifestyle characteristics'.[24] The ways in which these relationships cluster in British 'hard-to-let' estates leads to acute fear of social breakdown, because of the 'concentration of needy and vulnerable households'.[25]

More recent research by the York University Centre for Housing Policy[26] confirms that this pattern of **sink estates** is being repeated all over Britain: they found that as few as 22 per cent of heads of households in social housing had jobs. The best quality social housing stock had been sold to tenants with the 'right to buy', leaving a process of **reverse gentrification** whereby the worst social health and drug problems are being concentrated in a narrower social housing sector. Such research, and recent work on spatial patterns of crime in Merseyside (both reminiscent of the social disorganisation theories of the Chicago School) emphasise that lack of social cohesion 'may contribute to crime risks'.

POVERTY, CITIZENSHIP AND SOCIAL EXCLUSION

The discussion in this chapter has centred on a definition of poverty as relative. Poverty is not just about income level and absolute standards (of shelter and subsistence), it is about individuals whose lack of income excludes them from the accepted living patterns and activities of the society in which they live (see Townsend's definition on page 22). There is an important link, therefore, between poverty and the wider process of social exclusion.

> The notion of poverty is primarily focused upon *distributional* issues: the lack of resources at the disposal of an individual or household. In contrast, notions such as social exclusion focus primarily on *relational* issues, in other words, inadequate social participation, lack of social integration and lack of power.[27] (emphasis added)

According to such views, while poverty is an outcome of 'lack of disposable income', social exclusion is a more dynamic and multi-faceted process: it involves a 'breakdown of the major social systems ... that should guarantee full citizenship'.[28] So, what is citizenship? Citizenship, according to T H Marshall,[29] comprises three essential elements:

- the civil
- the political
- the social.

The first is associated with the rule of law and includes freedom of speech and the right to justice. The second concerns the ability to participate in politics (by voting or standing for office). The third includes:

> ... the whole range from the right to a modicum of economic welfare and security to the right to share in the full social heritage and to live the life of a civilised being according to the standards prevailing in the society.[30]

By examining the meaning of full citizenship we gain an insight into the links between poverty, citizenship and social exclusion. Figure 2.2 demonstrates the ways in which full citizenship is denied by a range of inequalities which are civil, political, social and environmental. For example, criminal victimisation, restrictions in legal aid, unemployment, low pay, welfare benefit cuts, water debt, illness and geographies of despair can all serve to deny the poor the experience of full citizenship. In other words, 'poverty is corrosive of citizenship'.[31]

But poverty is not the *only* condition which leads to social exclusion. Many British citizens are excluded from full civil, political and social participation through institutional racism.[32] The growing incidence of racial harassment and attacks shows that for many Black subjects, even the basic 'negative' right to walk the streets freely, without fear or harassment, is illusory. But, where poverty coincides with these wider dimensions of social exclusion, the effects are compounding, especially for poorer women and for members of minority ethnic groups (see Chapters 6 and 7).

Figure 2.2: **Citizenship: dimensions and denials**

Dimensions of citizenship	Denials
Civil and political rights	
Freedom of speech and association	• Criminal victimisation • Racial harassment • Public order legislation and civil liberties (to assemble and protest)
Freedom from discrimination Protection of the law (for self and property)	• Limited political participation • Erosion of legal rights ('right' to counsel; 'right' to fair trial and to trial by jury; 'right to silence')
Social and economic rights Education Housing Health care To own property To consume goods and services Work and participation in economic life To an income (welfare rights)	• Inequities in social provision of education, health care, housing, and social amenities • Unemployment • Underemployment and low pay • Erosion of benefit levels • Restricted access to welfare benefits (targeting and desert) • Policing of (and for) the family
Environmental rights To the benefits, in amenity and health, of a safe and clean environment	• Poverty, sickness and disease • Geographies of despair • Urban and rural pollution • Water debt (post privatisation)

THE RIGHTS AND DUTIES OF THE 'GOOD CITIZEN'

Even this brief discussion of citizenship has shown that many individuals and groups are effectively excluded from enjoying the rights of fully social citizenship. But, from the 'right' of the political spectrum, citizenship is primarily a matter of give and take: if you want to **take** advantage of the 'rights' of citizenship, you must **give**, by exercising the duties and responsibilities that accompany it. In the 1990s the issue of what **rights** a citizen may expect has been seen in fairly minimalist terms. To the extent that they exist at all, these rights have often been expressed in terms of 'customer charters' which centre on minimum standards of service for a variety of customers – whether hospital patients, parents of school children or rail travellers.

But this means that rights are attached to the status of 'customer'. The more customer-power you possess, the more rights you can enjoy. For one of the least powerful groups in society – social security claimants – the issue of rights is yet more problematic. As we have seen (in Chapter 1), social security reforms have over the past two decades undercut the very concept of 'welfare rights'. Although the Benefits Agency currently publishes a *Customers Charter*, the rights it (allegedly) guarantees can be regarded as tokenistic and purely administrative – as, for example, the 'rights' to have your telephone calls dealt with as promptly as possible, and to have your income support claim dealt with within 13 days. Even these minimal thresholds become meaningless if your **entitlement** to benefit is denied on grounds of desert, need, immigration status, availability for work or suspected fraud.

Citizenship is, therefore, a **conditional** status which depends upon several factors: being a *bona fide* customer; what level of rights the service deliverers are prepared (and able) to offer; being aware of what rights are guaranteed; and being able to exercise them and seek redress. But these are not the only conditional aspects of citizenship – another condition involves being a dutiful, good citizen. And so, in the 1990s, the 'give' aspects of the citizens' contract have been stressed at the expense of what they can 'take' from it – the emphasis has been more on the **duties** of active, independent, civic and responsible citizenship and less on meaningful **rights**.

So, who are dutiful citizens? In a nutshell, they are: economically independent; they obey the law; do not depend on the state for welfare; are 'good neighbours'; keep their homes in good repair; keep their children (and dogs) under control; are involved in the 'community' (perhaps through local political participation, neighbourhood watch, or voluntary work); and they pay their taxes.

MARGINALISATION AND RELATIVE DEPRIVATION

Being a good citizen means playing your part in the economy, as both a producer and a consumer. It therefore involves being economically productive (through work) and able to adopt (and so consume) the kinds of goods and services regarded as 'customary' for the society in which you live.[33] Being young, unemployed, disabled, a pensioner or lone parent family may therefore mean exclusion from fully social citizenship – it certainly means economic marginalisation. In turn, marginalisation is closely linked with the concept of relative deprivation.

According to Young and Lea,[34] 'relative deprivation is the excess of expectations over opportunity'. It involves not only economic and political marginality, but a feeling of frustration at the blocked opportunities which are felt to prevent full participation in social life. It is both the awareness of, and frustration at, the **relative** nature of this deprivation which is crucial in shaping how individuals respond. Both can arise from living, literally, alongside examples of conspicuous consumption – as in the case of the 1980s 'yuppie' London Docklands development, which starkly contrasted with the extreme poverty of other Eastenders in surrounding areas.

This awareness and frustration, which may lead to a sense of relative deprivation, can also arise from heightened expectations. For most families and young people the styles of living, dress, culture and consumption they aspire to are defined and fuelled by the media (especially television and advertising). But, more often than not, these aspirations are completely at odds with their lived experience and their life chances. Apparently, expensive perfume, designer clothes, high-style home furnishings, gourmet food and drink, state-of-the-art TVs, out-of-this-world domestic appliances, computers, sports gear, toys, fast cars and slim, sexy partners are all 'on offer' to anyone who wants, and tries hard enough, to attain them.

But this version of the 'American Dream' of success is not realisable for most Britons in the late 1990s. For some who find that their **legitimate** opportunities to make the dream come true are blocked, **illegitimate** means, involving crime, may be one option. Nonetheless, it is crucial to stress that while crime may be the chosen option for some, it is by no means an inevitable or universal response to poverty and relative deprivation. In this sense, **poverty should be seen as a source, rather than a cause, of crime**.[35]

DOES UNEMPLOYMENT CAUSE CRIME?

In commonsense terms the notion that unemployment causes crime can traditionally be seen from two different perspectives: first, it can reflect the age-old saying that 'the devil makes work for idle hands'. This adage reinforces the notion that crime is the product of idleness and so is predominantly committed by the poor. Secondly, it may reflect the alternative saying that 'needs must when the devil drives', which signals a reluctant acceptance that crime is committed by the unemployed, as an inevitable response to their poverty.

But, beyond mere 'commonsense' there are many other ways of conceptualising the crime–unemployment relationship. One alternative argument is that unemployment causes crime not merely out of economic necessity, but as a more complex expression of the relative deprivation, despair and social exclusion felt by the unemployed. This view was echoed in the evidence offered by John Wells to the 1994 House of Commons Select Committee on Employment.

> Mass unemployment on the scale which the UK has experienced since the late 1970s and increasing relative inequality in income and wealth *must surely* lead to an erosion of individual and moral constraint on unlawful behaviour – not necessarily confined to the unemployed themselves but spread more widely in the community ... An advanced industrial system that operates permanently under conditions of mass unemployment risks losing legitimacy and acceptability amongst large numbers of its citizens – the more so when members of the ruling elite appear to enjoy huge rewards which cannot be related to their productivity. The rising tide of crime and delinquency *must* owe something to the breakdown of this social compact ... to a growing sense of unfairness and to the stifling of potential represented by unemployment.[36] (emphasis added)

The added dimension which Wells presents here is that crime is not *just* committed by the poor and the unemployed, but that growing social inequality fosters a sense of unfairness and injustice at the undeserved rewards of the rich – some of which may well have been gained illicitly. This 'breakdown' in the social compact makes it more likely that the rich will commit crime too. This is a crucial argument, and one we must not lose sight of (see Chapters 3 and 6). It is also in line with the view, persuasively expressed by Steven Box,[37] that while it is too simplistic to argue that 'poverty causes crime', **widening income inequality** could be linked with rates of criminal activity. Clearly this criminal activity can be undertaken by the rich as well as the poor.

What evidence is there for an 'unemployment causes crime'

hypothesis? There has been no shortage of research in this area, which has been summarised by criminologists from Europe and the USA.[38] But the conclusions arising from this research are equivocal and display a 'consensus of doubt' about the connection between rising unemployment and rising crime rates.[39] While, in Wells' words, there is a widespread belief that there 'must surely' be a relationship between the economy, widening social inequality and crime rates, the exact nature of that relationship is still unclear. (But see Chapter 4 for a discussion of the relationship between the **economy** and **rates of imprisonment**, which is probably a clearer one.)

Some commentators who deny *any* causal link between unemployment rates and crime rates cite the example of Britain in the 1930s in their defence. If, they argue, mass unemployment leads to rising crime, then the unemployment rates of the 1930s would have generated a massive explosion of criminal activity – it did not. Therefore, if the mass unemployment of the 1930s did not cause a crime wave, surely we cannot now 'blame' the crime rates of the 1980s and '90s on unemployment.

But critics of this view would counter that we cannot compare the 1930s and the 1980s and '90s. What distinguished the situation of the unemployed in these periods is the different **beliefs** they held about the causes and consequences of unemployment. In the 1930s, the unemployed regarded their situation as essentially temporary – they had had some experience of work in their near past and hoped to have jobs again in the near future. They were also more resigned to their position in a relatively fixed (and segregated) social class structure, where relative deprivation was not acutely felt. But, in the 1980s and '90s the unemployed often have little or no experience of full-time work; have no faith that they will gain such experience in the foreseeable future; and are acutely aware of their relatively deprived status.[40]

Others argue that it is possible to identify a link between crime rates and the **boom and recession cycles of the economy**. For instance, Field[41] argued that while economic recession is linked with crimes of property, crimes of violence can be associated with economic prosperity. Based on an analysis of data for England and Wales throughout the twentieth century, Field argued that as spending power increases quickly, the longer-term increase in property crime slows down. When personal consumption becomes static or declines, property crime rises again. By contrast, he saw violent crime associated with economic prosperity (a view which was congruent with the 1990s moral panic over the violent behaviour of 'lager louts'). But domestic violence was an exception, as it rose steeply when economic times were hard.

This theory was not popular in government circles where politicians were reluctant to acknowledge that crime was related to the economy (preferring to see it as the product of individual 'wickedness'). Consequently, the findings of this Home Office sponsored research were swiftly dismissed by the Home Office Minister, John Patten: when he was asked by journalists to comment on its findings, Patten asked a colleague if Mr Field was the member of staff 'who wore an earring'.[42] Subsequent Home Office research on this issue has proved less controversial.

Nonetheless, there are many difficulties with a theory which sees the economy as a determining factor in crime rates. First, the exception of (reported) domestic violence proves the rule – that no 'macro' level theory of crime is comprehensive. Secondly, there is no place in this explanation for considering non-property crime. Crimes which are not committed for financial gain – for example, vandalism, 'joyriding' and drug (ab)use – cannot easily be explained within a purely economic framework. But, at the same time, this framework ignores many of the most costly financial crimes (committed by and for businesses) which cannot be read off as the product of poverty and recession: on the contrary, they exploded in the 'boom' of the 1980s.

As will be argued in Chapter 3, the extent and seriousness of business crime is the clearest evidence against the 'unemployment causes crime' hypothesis. While unemployment and relative deprivation do form part of the social landscape in which crime is committed, we need to remember that:

- the research on the links between crime and unemployment is often **contradictory**;
- research is invariably based on **reported or known crime** (which has serious implications for the neglect of hidden crimes such as domestic violence, racial harassment and business or white-collar crime);
- any explanation of crime which focuses on the economy may **'miss' the individual level** where the decision whether to opt for crime is made;
- following on from this, this type of theory is **deterministic**: but,

not all individuals respond in the same ways to the same economic and social circumstances (put simply, not all the unemployed turn to crime);

• finally, most established research on the links between unemployment and crime has been geared to the unemployment and crimes of *men*: it **fails to take account of female crimes**, largely because levels of female crime and unemployment are not seen to 'count'.[43]

Turning from the issue of unemployment and crime, the wider links between issues of gender, poverty and crime will now be addressed through an examination of one classic 'crime of poverty' – prostitution.

CRIMES OF POVERTY: PROSTITUTION

Materially, prostitution is often a response to poverty, financial hardship and need ... As a response to poverty, selling sex is often a last resort, the body one's last commodity. We cannot look at prostitution without looking at the social and economic contexts which give rise to it. The majority of women's work is part time, low status and low paid. There is an absence of good quality child care facilities. There is an increasing number of young people, disenfranchised, disaffected and homeless.[44]

O'Neill neatly summarises the results of contemporary research about the relationship between poverty and prostitution. Prostitution is itself not a crime – but soliciting for trade is. In other words, the law accepts the existence of prostitution, but criminalises prostitutes. The law itself is mainly concerned with regulating (usually female) street prostitution and it formally identifies the women involved in this trade as 'common prostitutes'.[45] Although prostitution is discussed here as a **crime of poverty**, it can be persuasively argued that it is also a crime which **further impoverishes** the majority of women who engage in it.

Recent research conducted by Jo Phoenix[46] offers a unique insight into the lives of 21 women involved in prostitution and demonstrates many of the paradoxes which characterise their lives. These women describe their entry into (or return to) prostitution in terms of several factors which interlock around their experiences of poverty:

- **'no one would employ me':** a lack of opportunity (and qualifications) for legitimate work;
- **'sorting out' poverty:** a rational response to living on inadequate social security benefits;
- **'looking out for each other':** the effects of single parenthood, poverty and stigmatisation (seeing prostitution as an alternative community and social support network);
- **housing problems, homelessness and 'doing a runner':** prostitution as a response to personal and housing crises;
- **rejecting dependency:** prostitution as a strategy for independence – from local authority care, from (often violent) men and from state welfare.

In offering these rationales for prostitution, the women interviewed were aware of several paradoxes. Although it was seen as a way of 'sorting out' poverty, prostitution, more often than not, trapped them in a cycle of continuing financial and housing crises.

> Most of the women represented involvement in prostitution as a financial trap which created further problems and risks rather than as a means of achieving economic and social survival and stability ... In terms of both income [and risk] involvement in prostitution was *extremely costly.*[47]

Housing crises often arose on leaving care or because of the need to escape from violent partners. On the one hand, these women presented prostitution as a strategy for independence and survival, for themselves and their children. But, on the other hand, it often entailed another kind of dependence on (often violent) men who acted as pimps.

In addition to the substantial risks of victimisation and personal health involved in prostitution, there are economic risks too. These are summarised by Phoenix in three themes:

- starting up;
- 'revolving doors';
- the 'easy money' myth.

First, 'starting up' in prostitution requires an obvious financial investment (ranging from clothes and condoms to a mobile phone and flat rental). As one 18-year-old told Phoenix, 'You end up paying more to go to work than you end up earning.' Secondly, this situation is exacerbated by a criminal justice system which acts as a 'revolving door' in processing prostitutes, because the typical sentence for loitering or soliciting is a fine. Thousands of pounds worth of fines can be accrued by some prostitutes, who may then make the rational economic decision to go to prison for fine default rather that pay.[48] The obvious irony is that in sentencing the 'common prostitute' to a financial penalty, magistrates are reinforcing a vicious circle, which forces these women back into prostitution to pay their fines, or forces them into prison.

The 'revolving doors' syndrome is also evident in recent statistics on prostitution-related arrests in the Wolverhampton Division of the West Midlands police force. In 1991 it was estimated that the prostitution 'problem' in Wolverhampton ranked third largest in the country. Arrest data for the last three years for 'loitering for the purposes of prostitution' is as follows:

1993	2,242 arrests involving 202 individual women
1994	2,225 arrests involving 221 individual women
1995	1,967 arrests involving 205 individual women

In 1995 only 100 of the 205 women arrested for loitering were prosecuted (as a result of offending on more than two occasions). But it is clear that the *same* women are being repeatedly processed through the revolving doors of the criminal justice system. Moreover, in 1995, 17 of these women entered prison through the 'back door' as fine defaulters, although this was a significant reduction on the figure of 91 women who had been imprisoned for defaulting on prostitution-related fines in 1994.[49]

Thirdly, and not surprisingly, the 'easy money' which prostitution is seen to yield is illusory. It is not only repeated fines which destroy this illusion: the income gained from prostitution is unofficial, undeclared and cannot provide the basis for any sound financial future. It holds no possibility for deferred benefits (for sickness and old age) and has no 'borrowing value' (for mortgages or hire purchase). Taken together, Phoenix concludes that the harsh realities and the practices of prostitution offer no solution to poverty but, rather, lead to further impoverishment of the women involved.

CRIMES OF POVERTY: SOCIAL SECURITY FRAUD

Social security fraud can be regarded as another illegitimate response to living in poverty. If welfare benefits are not adequate to meet needs, then fiddling the system may, for some, present a way of making ends meet. Fiddling often takes the form of working 'on the side', in the hidden or casual sectors of the economy.[50] Ironically, benefit fraud involving 'doing the double' by working and claiming helps to maintain a vulnerable, disposable workforce for the informal labour market. This, in turn, reproduces the very constraints (of unemployment, casual and poorly paid jobs) which keeps claimants in the benefit and poverty traps. Recent research confirms that although individual motivations for benefit fraud are multiple and complex, the over-arching reason is one of economic necessity.[51]

Other justifications offered for fraud refer to claimant's dis-empowered status and to the vagaries of the benefit system itself. Being 'messed about' by the system and a feeling of 'justified disobedience' (in a society where 'everyone fiddles') played a significant part in the rationales offered by social security fraudsters for their actions.[52]

Of course, not all social security fraud is the product of *individual* responses to poverty and the 'swings and roundabouts' of the benefits system. A proportion of fraud is large-scale and more akin to organised crimes. These can include multiple identity frauds, forgery of order books and giros and housing benefit frauds by landlords. Nevertheless, the vast majority of *known* fraud falls into the 'individual' category (but see Chapter 5 for a fuller discussion of estimates of the scale of benefit fraud). In addition, the perception of staff working in local Benefits Agency offices is that most social security frauds are disorganised crimes of need rather than organised crimes of greed. Moreover, most social security claimants themselves distinguish between what they see as acceptable and unacceptable fiddling. In this context, organised frauds which are *not* motivated by poverty are regarded as 'unacceptable'.[53]

Chapter 5 will examine the regulation and punishment of social security fraud in more detail. At this point it is worth noting that acknowledging benefit fraud as a crime of poverty does not mean **condoning** it, but does reflect an **understanding** of the circum-stances in which it is most likely to be committed (and, in so doing, signposts the starting point for any sensible anti-fraud policy). These circumstances include:

- well-documented widening of social and economic inequality, in general;
- declining relative value of means-tested benefits, in particular;

- the vagaries, 'swings and roundabouts' of a complex benefits system (see Chapter 5);
- narrowing (legitimate) options for economic independence;
- the stigmatising effects of the 'scrounger mythology' (see Chapter 6);
- the cumulative effects of all of the above in generating and reinforcing social exclusion.

SUMMARY

This chapter has looked at how poverty, deprivation and citizenship have been conceptualised and at changes in the distribution of income and wealth over the past two decades. It has also examined suggestions of a causal link between poverty and crime, and unemployment and crime. But the evidence for these links is contradictory: certainly the theory that unemployment causes crime is a highly dubious one.

Although poverty may appear to **cause** crime, it is more appropriately seen as a **source** of crime: the examples of prostitution and social security fraud have been termed 'crimes of poverty', but it needs to be recognised that motivations for crime are complex. This is not to deny the impact of poverty on the lives and the opportunities of those who suffer it: for some, crime may be one response. But it may be chosen for a variety of reasons, which include:

- **an act of desperation:** the only way for those in debt to 'keep above water';
- **taking a chance:** a response to illegitimate opportunities;
- **nothing to lose:** the product of disillusionment and social exclusion;
- **a rational economic calculation:** given the limits of current benefit rates;
- the only means by which an individual can assert their **economic independence**;
- a product of **narrowing options**, for employment or social/personal stability.

As the next chapter will show, crime is not committed by the poor alone. Although official statistics, policing strategy, political speeches and media coverage all focus on 'poor crime', the most costly and the most serious crimes are perpetrated by the rich. In the light of this we need to critically re-evaluate how the relationships between poverty and crime are perceived.

NOTES

1   Joseph Rowntree Foundation, *Inquiry into Income and Wealth*, Vol 1, 1995.
2   K Joseph and J Sumption, *Equality*, J Murray, 1979, p27.
3   P Townsend, *Poverty in the United Kingdom*, Penguin, 1979, p31.
4   R Pryke, *Taking the Measure of Poverty*, IEA, 1995, p75.
5   King's Fund research, 1995.
6   A Walker and C Walker (eds), *The Growing Divide: a social audit 1979–87*, CPAG Ltd, 1987.
7   M Loney, 'A war on poverty or a war on the poor?', in *ibid*.
8   Quoted in J Rentoul, 'The new idle rich', in *New Statesman and Society*, 25 March 1988.
9   C Oppenheim and L Harker, *Poverty: the facts*, CPAG Ltd, 1996.
10 D Cook, *Rich Law, Poor Law: different responses to tax and supplementary benefit fraud*, Open University Press, 1989.
11 *Hansard*, 2 May 1991.
12 Joseph Rowntree Foundation, *Inquiry into Income and Wealth*, Vol 2, 1995, pp29, 57.
13 *Ibid*, pp61–2.
14 Low Pay Unit, *Low Pay Update*, Issue 2, 1996.
15 *See* note 1, p14.
16 *See* note 1, p15.
17 *See* note 12, p95.
18 *See* note 12, p105.
19 Oppenheim and Harker, *see* note 9; *Annual Abstract of Statistics*, HMSO, 1997
20 *Guardian*, 10 February 1997.
21 *Guardian*, 21 February 1997.
22 E Kempson *et al*, *Hard Times*, Policy Studies Institute, 1994.
23 *Ibid*; R Walker, 'The dynamics of poverty and social exclusion' in G Room (ed), *Beyond the Threshold: the measurement and analysis of social exclusion*, Policy Press, 1995.
24 A Hirschfield and K J Bowers, 'The development of a social demo-graphic and land use profiler of high crime', in *British Journal of Criminology*, Vol 37, No 1, Winter 1997, p104.
25 A Power and R Tunstall, *Swimming Against the Tide: polarisation and progress on 20 unpopular council estates, 1980–1995*, Joseph Rowntree Foundation, 1995, p4.
26 Hirschfield and Bowers, *see* note 24.
27 G Room, 'Poverty and social exclusion: the new European agenda for policy and research' in G Room (ed), *see* note 23, p5.

28 J Berghman, 'Social exclusion in Europe: policy context and analytical framework', in G Room (ed), *see* note 23, p20.

29 T H Marshall, *The Right to Welfare and Other Essays*, Henemann, 1981.

30 *Ibid*, p10.

31 R Lister, *The Exclusive Society: citizenship and the poor*, CPAG Ltd, 1990.

32 D Cook, 'Racism, citizenship and exclusion', in B Hudson and D Cook (eds), *Racism and Criminology*, Sage, 1993.

33 Townsend, *see* note 3; Lister, *see* note 31.

34 J Young and J Lea, *What's To Be Done About Law and Order?*, Pluto Press, 2nd edn, 1993, p218.

35 J Reiman, *The Rich Get Rich and the Poor Get Prison*, Macmillan, 1990.

36 Wells, quoted in D Downes, 'What the next government should do about crime', in *The Howard Journal*, Vol 36, No 1, 1997, p5.

37 S Box, *Recession, Crime and Punishment*, Macmillan, 1987.

38 Council of Europe, *Economic Crisis and Crime*, European Committee on Crime Problems, 1985; Box, *ibid*; Chiricos, 'Rates of crime and unemployment: an analysis of aggregate research evidence', in *Social Problems*, Vol 34, 1987; S Field, *Trends in Crime and Their Interpretation: a study of recorded crime in England and Wales*, Home Office Research Study 119/90, Home Office, 1990.

39 B Hudson, *Penal Policy and Social Justice*, Macmillan, 1993, p69.

40 Box, *see* note 37; Young and Lea, *see* note 34; Downes,*see* note 36.

41 Field, *see* note 38.

42 *Guardian*, 29 September 1990.

43 Naffine and Gale, 'Testing and Nexus: crime, gender and unemployment', in *British Journal of Criminology*, Vol 29, No 2, 1989.

44 M O'Neill, 'Prostitute women now', in A Scambler and G Scambler (eds), *Re-Thinking Prostitution: purchasing sex in the 1990s*, Routledge, 1997, p12.

45 S Edwards, 'Prostitutes: victims of law, social policy and organised crime', in P Carlen and A Worrall (eds), *Gender, Crime and Justice*, Open University Press, 1987; O'Neill, *ibid*.

46 J Phoenix, 'Making Sense of Prostitution Today', unpublished PhD thesis, University of Bath, 1997, forthcoming.

47 *Ibid*.

48 Edwards, *see* note 45; Phoenix, *see* note 46.

49 *Wolverhampton Crime Audit*, 1996.

50 D Cook, 'Fiddling tax and benefits: inculpating the poor, exculpating the rich', in P Carlen and D Cook (eds), *Paying for Crime*, Open University Press, 1989.

51 H Dean and M Melrose, 'Manageable discord: fraud and resistance in the social security system', in *Social Policy and Administration*, Vol 31, No 2, 1997.

52 *Ibid*.

53 Cook, *see* note 50; Dean and Melrose, *see* note 51.

3 Crime problems

INTRODUCTION: WHAT IS CRIME?

This may seem a simple question, but it is not so simply answered. One basic definition is that a crime is a violation of the law of the land which is liable to official punishment. Under this definition it becomes clear that what makes an act criminal does not depend on the quality of the act itself, but on how it is defined by society and **the law**. For example, homicide would seem a clearly criminal act, but it can be defined in a variety of ways depending upon who commits it, and under what circumstances. For instance, it is acceptable to kill in times of war (providing, of course, that the 'rules' of war are themselves obeyed); in certain societies it is permissible to help others to die, while in others this is considered murder; legal rules of provocation and diminished responsibility can mean that the identical act of taking another's life may be defined very differently if the perpetrator is a man or a woman, young or very old, considered sane or mentally ill.

Changes in the law are continually redefining crime. The 1960s saw abortion, attempted suicide and male homosexual activity (by those aged 21 or more) de-criminalised. But the law on consent in the 1990s means that homosexual males between the ages of 16 and 18 may be regarded as committing a criminal act by expressing their sexuality, while their heterosexual counterparts are not. New legislation covering areas as diverse as public order, labour law, child support, pornography and 'dangerous dogs' have all generated new offences, as have recent technological advances in computing and communications. Crime is therefore a changing category, and one which is **relative** to the values and concerns of the society in which it is so defined.

Crime encompasses a wide range of offences which vary in seriousness. But when thinking about crime in popular terms, there is a tendency to think of the more serious offences against the person and against property. While most individuals have little direct experience of serious crime, those who have suffered victimisation are bound to find their views about crime and punishment influenced by personal experience. But for many of us, our perceptions of crime are shaped by the 'second hand' experiences of friends and neighbours, and by the extensive media coverage of crime which affects us all. However, according to 'realist' commentators, people's conceptions of crime are rooted in rational concerns which reflect their material experiences, and not in mass media 'fantasies' about crime.[1] Alternatively, some would go as far as to argue that 'it is no longer possible to discuss crime without talking about the media, and vice versa'.[2]

Crime has long been regarded as, by definition, a **newsworthy** topic.[3] Violent crime, in particular, represents a classic negative, atypical, unifying and unambiguous event. But not all crimes are equal in terms of their news value because not all types of crime are readily translated into simple, personalised and hard-hitting stories. For example, while we can all readily identify with the graphic pictures and accounts of victims of violent crime, it is less easy to construct stories about complex frauds or health and safety violations to achieve the same impact. This chapter will go on to examine the invisibility of these 'white-collar crimes' in the official crime statistics, the criminal justice process, the media and in popular 'fears' about crime. As Bauer pointedly remarked:

> White-collar crime is not really the subject of public fear. Nobody ever felt threatened by embezzling from a bank. We will need to get the public mad about white-collar crime as well.[4]

Given the scale and seriousness of such offences, there is a great deal for the public to 'get mad' about! (Chapter 4 will look in more detail at such issues together with the policing and punishment of white collar crimes, and Chapter 6 will examine which crimes people *say* they are afraid of.)

When it comes to reporting crime and punishment, media institutions do not operate in a vacuum: they are driven by news values and also by news sources. The starting point for much crime and punishment copy is an 'official' pronouncement of some kind.

These official statements, in turn, draw on official criminal statistics and criminal cases to demonstrate the concerns of the commentator. As a result, it is those police officers, judges and magistrates, Home Office ministers and MPs who have access to **official knowledge** who effectively shape the **crime agenda,** which the media reproduces. The agenda is mainly set in terms of 'traditional crimes' and stereotyped criminals – in other words violent, 'street' and property crime committed by the poor.

In order to understand how the crime agenda (and the crime 'problem') is defined, we need first to examine how official knowledge about crime and punishment is produced. This chapter will seek to do this by addressing three fundamental questions:

- What **counts** as crime?
- **What** do we think we know about crime?
- What **don't** we know about crime and punishment?

In exploring these questions, we will examine how the popular crime agenda affects the ways we think about poverty, crime and punishment. We will then go on to raise the following alternative set of questions which imply very different ways of viewing the crime 'problem':

- Who **commits** crime?
- Who **suffers** most as a result of crime?
- Who **gets caught** and prosecuted, and why?

OFFICIAL STATISTICS: WHAT COUNTS AS CRIME?

There are three kinds of lies: lies, damned lies and statistics. (Disraeli)

This cautionary remark by a nineteenth century Prime Minister shows that the (ab)use of statistics has always been a problem for policy-makers. Given that crime is such a controversial topic, the problems posed by criminal statistics are all the more acute. The official measure of crime in England and Wales (Scotland and Northern Ireland have distinctive legal systems) is provided in the Home Office Criminal Statistics. These represent all **notifiable offences recorded by the police.** However, it is essential to disentangle the two different processes at work when counting:

- **notifiable** and
- **recorded** offences.

First, according to the Home Office, the term **notifiable offences** 'broadly covers the more serious offences', although they acknowledge that some crimes may be notifiable because of the legal category in which they fall, and not because of their seriousness.[5] For instance, if a child forcibly takes something from another child this could, if reported, be counted as robbery (a serious and notifiable offence). But many offences which may popularly be seen as part of the 'crime problem' are *not* notifiable: as a result, many non-notifiable offences arising from neighbourhood disturbances, disorderly behaviour and late night drink-related incidents do not officially contribute to the local or national crime picture. Similarly, there are a series of offences relating to public order, prostitution and the possession of cannabis which have a serious and high media profile, but which are not included in the list of notifiable offences. When discussing crime trends it is therefore vital to remember exactly what *is* being counted, and what is not.

Secondly, the process of actually **recording** these offences involves a series of decisions which can lead to the counting *in* or the counting *out* of crimes (summarised in Figure 3.1). As far as the police are concerned:

> Decisions need to be taken about whether a reported offence did actually occur and whether it is appropriate to record it; it might arise, for example, in the apparent theft of small sums of money. A broken window might be an accident, criminal damage or attempted burglary … In other cases, decisions have to be made about whether a group of offenders were acting together, whether a series of incidents formed one continuous offence, whether different offences in one incident should be counted separately and so on.[6]

These decisions are also shaped by **where** an incident occurs. Most of the crimes committed by and for business are committed in private places, are **invisible** and the victims unaware that they have taken place. Where violent crime is concerned, an assault involving serious physical injury in the **private** arena of the home is less likely to be reported than one taking place in a **public** place, where bystanders may witness the offence. Even then, the decision of a witness to report an offence is influenced by a variety of factors: if the crime is regarded as a 'victimless crime' (involving, for example, prostitution or drug abuse), the observer may be less willing to report it; if a victim or witness knows the offender, s/he may be unwilling to come forward; a witness may fear intimidation or may not want 'to get involved'; not everyone who witnesses an incident may see it as a crime (this can depend on their own perception, tolerance and knowledge of unlawful behaviour); and a witness or victim may consider the offence too trivial to report.

The decisions of victims and bystanders to report incidents are to some extent shaped by their faith in the police. If relations between the police and community are poor, or if the victim or bystander has had a negative experience with the police in the past, they may be less willing to report. Another influence on reporting practices can be a sense of resignation – the belief that the police cannot do anything to solve the crime anyway, so 'why bother reporting it?'[7] This can be compounded if there is no incentive to report, as in the case of a repeated burglary where the victim is not insured and has nothing to gain by reporting the offence. Where there is an insurance incentive, as in the case of car theft and insured household burglaries, there is a far higher rate of reporting.[8]

Negative expectations of the police can play a significant part in the decisions of women and Black victims to report crime (or not). Where they perceive these crimes to be racially motivated, the satisfaction of minority groups with police responses is even lower than for other types of offence.[9]

The recording process starts when someone reports a crime to the police, or when the police discover that an offence has been committed. If there is initial (*prima facie*) evidence that an offence has been committed, a crime report will be completed. But subsequent factors may lead to changes in this initial report – an offender's age may change the classification of an offence; criminal damage may be costed at less than £20 (and so not notifiable); further inquiries or evidence may reveal that no offence was actually committed. In addition, doubts about the validity and quality of a witness or victim's account may also lead to 'no-criming', and deletions from the crime statistics.

The cumulative result of this process is the figure of notifiable offences recorded by the police. In popular shorthand, this is **recorded crime**. This figure clearly does not reflect either the total number or the types of incidents which could, and should, be *counted as crime*. But this is the official 'recorded crime' figure which is published (quarterly) by the Home Office and announced and debated by politicians; forms the basis of analyses of crime trends over time; is reproduced in the media; and shapes public views about the nature and extent of crime.

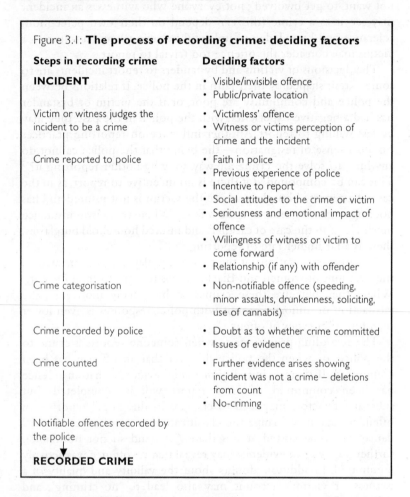

Figure 3.1: **The process of recording crime: deciding factors**

Steps in recording crime	Deciding factors
INCIDENT	• Visible/invisible offence
	• Public/private location
Victim or witness judges the incident to be a crime	• 'Victimless' offence
	• Witness or victims perception of crime and the incident
Crime reported to police	• Faith in police
	• Previous experience of police
	• Incentive to report
	• Social attitudes to the crime or victim
	• Seriousness and emotional impact of offence
	• Willingness of witness or victim to come forward
	• Relationship (if any) with offender
Crime categorisation	• Non-notifiable offence (speeding, minor assaults, drunkenness, soliciting, use of cannabis)
Crime recorded by police	• Doubt as to whether crime committed
	• Issues of evidence
Crime counted	• Further evidence arises showing incident was not a crime – deletions from count
	• No-criming
Notifiable offences recorded by the police	
RECORDED CRIME	

CRIME TRENDS: WHAT DO WE THINK WE KNOW ABOUT CRIME?

Tabloid headlines, politicians (notably those in opposition to the government of the day) and popular talk all proclaim a relentless increase in crime. The police, public and politicians often hark back to a 'golden age' (usually prior to the 'permissive sixties') when there was respect for law and order, and when the crime problem was far less pressing. But historical analysis tells us that every era claims 'things are getting worse' and longs for the mythical 'tranquillity of the past'.[10] Such 'respectable fears' are based on a mythical interpretation of this past. They are also reinforced by misleading analyses of crime trends.

At the extreme, such analyses can appeal very directly to populist, anecdotal and anti-academic prejudices. For example, in *Families Without Fatherhood*, the authors offer this vignette from pre-war Sunderland: a boy found having an illicit smoke was chased and caught by a policeman, and subsequently received 'a good telling off' by his father. This tale is held to exemplify the social control mechanisms of the day which were 'pervasive and consensual, and therefore low-key, good-humoured and effective'.[11] Those were the days!

In pursuing their argument about post-war family, moral and social decline, Dennis and Erdos go on to compare the theft of 50 cycles in Sunderland in 1938 with 1,438 cars stolen and burnt out in Tyne and Wear in 1990. The relative availability of bicycles and cars in 1938 and 1990 makes this comparison quite ridiculous. Nonetheless, they continue:

> In 1906 there had been 3,174 persons tried for burglary in the whole country; in 1992 in the Northumbria police area alone there were 159,000 cases of burglary, theft and robbery known to the police ... The total of reported crime increased in the single year 1989-90 for the single police area of Northumbria by a total in excess of the absolute limits of the variation of the conviction figures during the fifty year period 1857-1906 for the whole country.[12]

Comparisons like these undoubtedly achieve impact, but at the expense of validity and rationality – they fail to compare like with like. But by comparing 'apples with pears' these authors show that, as Disraeli was well aware, you can make statistics tell you (more or less) anything.

Long-term analysis of crime trends raises a series of problems. As we have seen, definitions of crime may change over time and new crimes are added to the statute book. Social attitudes to certain crimes (such as rape) and victims (who may be seen as 'asking for it') can shape reporting. But social change can also have an influence on the **opportunities** for certain types of crime, notably thefts and fraud: for instance, since the 1950s, the increasing availability of a wide range of portable consumer goods, from the 'transistor radio' to car stereos, VCRs and CD players, has increased such opportunities; and the development of new technologies has led to theft of, and crime using, computers, as well as an explosion in credit card ('plastic') fraud.

One way of tracing crime trends over time is to look at notifiable offences in relation to the size of the population. But even when expressed as a rate per 100,000 of the population, the figures still conceal unreported and non-notifiable offences and several changes to police recording practices. If we were to compare the crime rate of the 1990s with that of the 1950s, a dramatic picture would emerge. As Figure 3.2 demonstrates, this would indicate a *nine-fold* increase in recorded crime, and a crime rate (per 100,000 of the population) rising from 1,100 in 1950 to 9,500 in 1995. For all the reasons cited earlier – the criminalisation of more activities, consumer goods and credit crime – it is likely that property crime has increased significantly over the past 30 years. But all findings about crime trends should also be treated cautiously because they cannot take into account changes in policing practices and priorities.

As argued earlier, there is a shadowy figure of crime which remains entirely unknown to the police. It follows that policing resources may be targeted to shed light on certain areas and types of crime in the shadows. In other words, changes in policing strategy can illuminate the hidden figure of crime. But what is discovered depends on what area or type of crime has been highlighted. A blitz on 'street crime', for example, would undoubtedly lead to the discovery of criminal offences, although not necessarily the ones which it was intended to discover, as operation Swamp '81 in Brixton testified. This operation failed to reveal any street robberies – the crime it was targeted to find – but generated scores of arrests resulting from individual confrontations between young (predominantly Black) men and the police on the streets.[13]

The targeting of particular crimes and particular areas does not only reflect assumptions about the links between crime and poverty. It can also reflect what Keith termed the 'racialisation of the urban crisis'.[14] Operation Eagle Eye was launched in summer 1995 by the Metropolitan Police Commissioner, Sir Paul Condon, who voiced his belief that in London most 'muggers' were Black. A year on, the impact of Operation Eagle Eye on street robberies (which had increased by 14 per cent) was limited, but on relations with the

Figure 3.2: **Notifiable offences recorded by the police per 100,000 population 1950-1995**

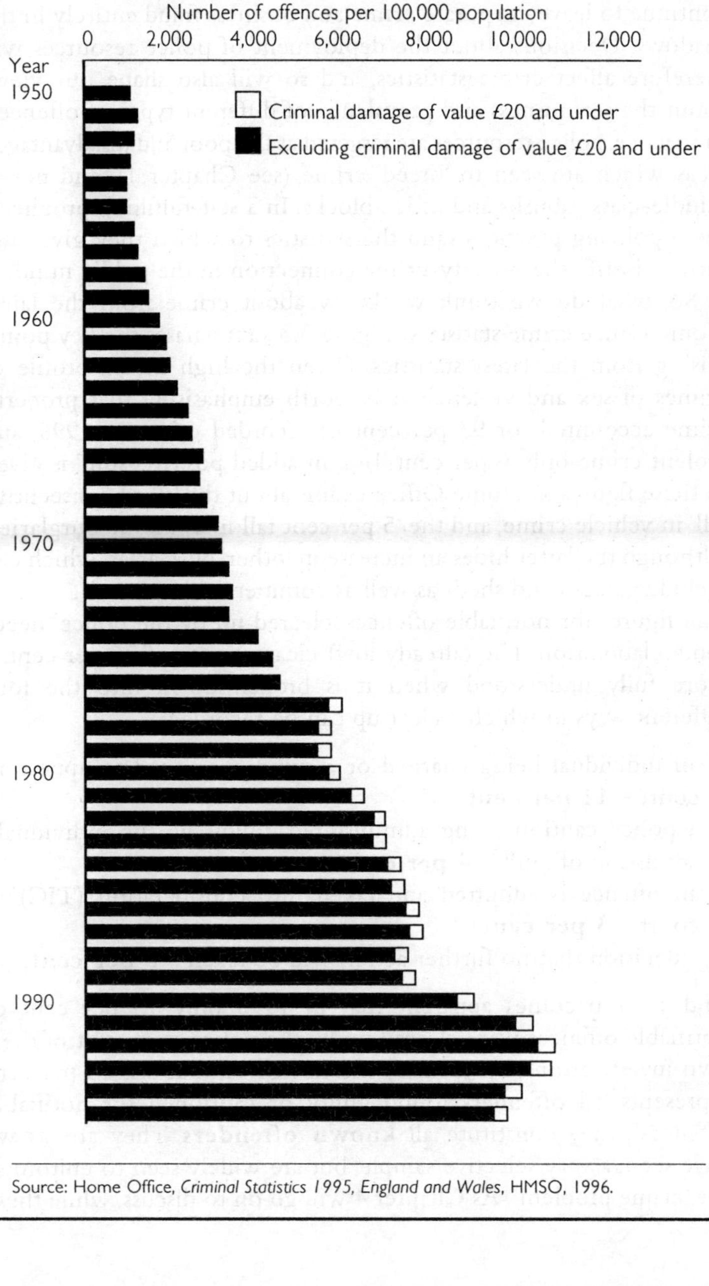

Number of offences per 100,000 population

☐ Criminal damage of value £20 and under

■ Excluding criminal damage of value £20 and under

Source: Home Office, *Criminal Statistics 1995, England and Wales*, HMSO, 1996.

Black community, it has had a more significant (and negative) impact.

It goes without saying that policing blitzes on street crime will continue to leave corporate crime and business fraud entirely in the shadows. Decisions about the deployment of police resources will therefore affect crime statistics, and so will also shape our views about the seriousness and prevalence of different types of offences. In practice, police resources are targeted at the poor and disadvantaged areas which are seen to 'breed' crime (see Chapter 1), and not at middle-class suburbs and office blocks. In a self-fulfilling prophecy, these policing practices (and the statistics to which they give rise) further justify the poverty-crime connection in the public mind.

So, what do we think we know about crime from the latest Home Office crime statistics? Figure 3.3 summarises the key points arising from the latest statistics. Given the high media profile of crimes of sex and violence, it is worth emphasising that property crime accounted for 93 per cent of recorded crime in 1995, and violent crime only 6 per cent. But an added positive 'spin' is given to these figures in Home Office claims about the 'third consecutive fall' in vehicle crime, and the '5 per cent fall in domestic burglaries' (although the latter hides an increase in 'other' burglaries, which can include garages and sheds as well as commercial premises!).

The figures for notifiable offences 'cleared up by the police' needs some elaboration. The (already low) clear up rate of 26 per cent is more fully understood when it is broken down into the four different ways in which a clear up can be recorded:

- an individual being charged or a summons issued to appear in court – **11 per cent**
- a police caution being administered, following the individual's admission of guilt – **4 per cent**
- an offence is admitted and taken into consideration (TIC) in court – **3 per cent**
- a decision that no further action will be taken – **8 per cent**.

And so it becomes apparent that in 1995 only 15 per cent of notifiable offences were cleared up by the police as a result of their own investigations, by 'primary means'. Given that this 15 per cent represents 'all offenders found guilty or cautioned for notifiable offences', they constitute all **known offenders**. They are, as we have seen, a very selective sample, but are widely seen to epitomise the 'crime problem'. As Chapter 4 will go on to discuss, while these may be the **identikit** criminals who go on to fill our prisons, they cannot be said to accurately reflect all those individuals who **commit** crime.

Figure 3.3: **Notifiable offences recorded by the police, 1995: key points**

- 5.1 million notifiable offences were recorded by the police in 1995, a fall of 3 per cent over 1994
- 4.7 million (93 per cent) of these offences were against property (including burglary, theft, criminal damage and fraud)
- Violent crime accounted for 6 per cent of all notifiable offences in 1995. Crimes of violence (violence against the person, sexual offences and robbery) showed a marginal increase (of 0.2 per cent) over the previous year, the smallest increase in 30 years
- Within the category of violent crime, violence against the person and sexual offences fell by 3 per cent and 5 per cent respectively, but robberies rose by 13 per cent over the previous year
- Vehicle crime fell by 5 per cent (to 1.3 million offences) in 1995, the third consecutive annual fall
- Burglaries fell by 1 per cent (to 1.2 million offences) in 1995: this incorporated a 5 per cent fall in domestic burglaries
- Between 1985 and 1995 the recorded crime rate per 100,000 of the population increased from 7,300 to 9,900
- Between 1985 and 1995, recorded crime rose by 41 per cent (by an average of 3.5 per cent per year)
- 26 per cent of notifiable offences were cleared up by the police in 1995

Source: Home Office, *Criminal Statistics 1995, England and Wales*, HMSO, 1996.

WHAT *DON'T* WE KNOW ABOUT CRIME AND PUNISHMENT?

As we have seen, the official crime statistics are largely shaped by police definitions of incidents, police recording practices and policing strategies. What these statistics do not reveal is the perspective of the victim. From the 1960s, victim surveys were conducted in the USA and provided an impetus for subsequent British studies. The government's *General Household Survey* had since the 1970s (inter-mittently) asked questions about whether or not respondents had been burgled. But from 1982, the Home Office has conducted a series of large scale national victim report surveys – the *British Crime Surveys* (BCS). Six 'sweeps' have been conducted between 1982 and 1996. In 1996 over 16,000 adults were interviewed about their experience of criminal victimisation in the previous year.[15]

The BCS was to serve three purposes:

- to compliment official crime statistics, and add to knowledge about how these are constructed;
- to act as an 'antidote' to popular misconceptions about crime by creating 'a more balanced climate of opinion about law and order';[16] *and*
- to offer a fresh source of information for criminological research.

In relation to the second aim the BCS has had paradoxical effects. On the one hand it sought to combat the 'irrational fear of crime' by demonstrating that the 'real' risks of serious crime were very low. But, on the other hand, when its results were compared with the police figures, the BCS uncovered a huge amount of unknown and unrecorded crime. It therefore sent the mixed message that although there was much more crime than we officially 'knew' about, those individuals who worried most about crime (notably the elderly and women) should be reassured because they had the lowest statistical chances of being victims.

Chapter 6 will discuss the pitfalls in this rather over-simplified view of victimisation, but it is important here to establish *if* and *how* the BCS fills gaps in our knowledge about crime. In relation to its first aim, the BCS does offer some scope for comparison with the official crime statistics. Two-thirds of the offences reported in BCS fall into types which can be compared with police figures of recorded crime. These comparable sets of offences are:

- **acquisitive crime**: burglary, theft of or from vehicles, theft of a pedal cycle, theft from the person;
- **vandalism**: incidents of criminal damage against household property and vehicles;
- **violence**: wounding and robbery.

Although there are some marked discrepancies between police and BCS figures, it can be argued that the overall *direction* of changes in crime is not inconsistent.[17] While police figures indicated a fall in recorded crime of 8 per cent from 1993-95, the BCS indicated an overall rise of 2 per cent, but in some respects the 'gap' between

BCS and police figures is narrowing. Although this could be the result of improved reporting rates, it is important to stress that there is still significant under-reporting, even in cases of serious crime (see Table 3.1).

A comparison between the BCS estimates of crimes committed and police figures of recorded crime reveals that in 1995 there were:

- almost **three** times as many **domestic burglaries** committed as recorded;
- almost **four** times as many **bicycle thefts**;
- **four** times as many **thefts from vehicles**;
- **four** times as many **woundings**;
- **seven** times as many offences of **vandalism**
- **eight** times as many **robberies and thefts from the person**
- overall, **less than half** of BCS offences were recorded by the police.[18]

HIDDEN CRIMES: DOMESTIC VIOLENCE AND RACIAL HARASSMENT

The BCS also attempts to provide information on certain offences, such as **domestic violence**, which are grossly under-reported (and under-recorded) in official statistics. But the BCS admits that the measure it is able to provide is doubtful.[19] Domestic violence takes place in the private arena of the home, hidden from public view. Women (who are predominantly the victims) are often afraid to report those who are responsible for such violence – most often their male partners – and this fear can clearly influence reporting to the BCS as well as to the police. (It is also worth mentioning that the BCS sample is limited to households and so does not include women living in refuges.)

As far as police statistics are concerned, information on domestic violence is extremely problematic. Many incidents of domestic violence may fall far short of the legal definition of wounding and are not notifiable offences, though arguably they should be treated equally seriously. The notifiable offence of 'wounding' does involve a coding referring to the location of the offence (including 'domestic' locations), but not all incidents of wounding which take place in a home equate with domestic violence: for example, a quarrel between teenage friends in one of their homes could produce the category

TABLE 3.1: **Comparison of the results of the British Crime Survey with statistics of notifiable offences recorded by the police in England and Wales in 1995**

Offences	Notifiable offences recorded by the police		BCS best estimate of number committed (thousands)	Best estimate of percentage recorded
	Total (thousands)	Adjusted for comparison* (thousands)		
Violence against the person				
Wounding	203	174	860	20%
Other, not covered by BCS	9			
Burglary				
Burglary in a dwelling	644	644	1,754	37%
Other, not covered by BCS	596			
Robbery and theft from person	128	123	984	13%
Theft and handling of stolen goods				
Theft from vehicle (with loss)	715	657	2,522	26%
Theft or unauthorised taking of a motor vehicle with loss	431	402	499	81%
Theft from vehicle and attempted thefts or unauthorised taking of a motor vehicle (no loss)	176	150	1,291	12%
Theft of a pedal cycle	169	183	660	28%
Other, not covered by BCS	961			
Criminal damage	914	461	3,415	13%
Other, not covered by BCS	154			
Total	**5,100**	**2,794**	**11,986**	**23%**

* Adjustments necessary because of the sample structure and coverage of the BCS. Details of the adjustments are given in *1996 British Crime Survey (England and Wales) Technical Report*, SCPR, 1996.
Source: C Mirrlees-Black, P Mayhew and A Percy, *The 1996 British Crime Survey, England and Wales*, Home Office Statistical Bulletin 19/96, Home Office, 1996

of wounding in a dwelling, but this is entirely at odds with the conventional meaning of the term domestic violence.

Police forces have devoted specialist resources in an attempt to deal with these **hidden crimes**. In my locality, for example, the Wolverhampton (G Division of the West Midlands police force) Domestic Violence Unit collects data on the numbers of referrals they receive from police officers called out to 'domestic' incidents. Referral forms are filled in by police officers attending, irrespective of the call's outcome, and whether or not the victim wishes to proceed with the case. Figures for known incidents in Wolverhampton in 1994 and 1995 are given in Table 3.2. There is a very marked discrepancy between numbers of **known incidents** and numbers of **arrests**, with 1,992 incidents in 1995 and only 227 arrests. (This level of 'attrition rate' is not confined to cases of domestic violence – it is also evident in cases of sexual assaults where many victims are similarly fearful.)

TABLE 3.2: **Incidents of domestic violence in Wolverhampton: 1994 and 1995**

1994	Total incidents	1,870
	Advice/DVU follow up	1,336
	Refused to complain	190
	No further action	13
	Arrests	291
1995	Total incidents	1,992
	Advice/DVU follow up	1,865
	Refused to complain	215
	No further action	5
	Arrests	227
	Repeat victims	632

Note: Data refers to calendar years

Source: D Cook and M Roberts, *Wolverhampton Crime Audit 1994-96*, Wolverhampton Community Safety Partnership, 1996.

Because of the fear of reporting, the scale of the problem of domestic violence cannot be simply 'read-off' from these referral figures, even though they appear very high with almost 2,000 incidents recorded in the town in 1995, over half of which involved repeated victimisation. Nevertheless, these figures are still likely to represent the 'tip of the iceberg'. Given all of these reservations about the **under-reporting** of domestic violence, it is particularly telling that the figures indicate that in 1995 the *known* incidents of domestic violence in Wolverhampton were more than twice the figure for *all* recorded, notifiable offences of violence against the person in the town for 1995/96.

Another area of hidden crime surrounds **racially motivated offences**. The police record an incident as having a racial element if it appears to the reporting or investigating officer that the complaint involves an element of racial motivation, or if anyone else (including victim or bystanders) makes an allegation that racial motivation is involved. Police officers complete racial incident forms AT1 to record all such allegations. But problems of under-recording still arise if victims do not report such offences; if victims (and others) do not clearly make an allegation of racial motivation; or if police officers do not readily identify a complaint's racial element.

The Home Office report, *Racially Motivated Crime*,[20] included a comparison between BCS and police figures, finding that there was evidence of extensive under-reporting and recording of racially motivated incidents. For instance, in 1991 the police recorded 7,882 offences involving a racial element, while the BCS estimate for the same period was 130,000 racially motivated crimes and threats. Despite several problems of comparability with BCS figures, and the likelihood that the BCS too may underestimate 'lower level' harassment, it is clear that there is a significant problem in assessing the scale of racially motivated crime.

Police forms AT1 completed for racial incidents may be generated in a wide variety of circumstances, not just those of clear-cut 'race crime'. According to the *Wolverhampton Crime Audit*,[21] a total of 81 forms AT1 were completed in 1994, and 67 in 1995. However, this total of 148 racially motivated incidents over the two-year audit period is (as the Home Office report suggests), likely to grossly under-represent the scale of the problem of racially motivated crime in the town.

Hidden crimes, such as domestic violence, racial harassment, sexual offences and family abuse, may be under-reported and poorly recorded, even by victim surveys. Nevertheless, they are increasingly being placed on the crime agenda, not least because of vigorous campaigning by a variety of groups.

MISSING CRIMES

So, what crimes are missing from the official statistics, victim surveys and from the crime and campaigning agenda? To return to the quote from Bauer at the beginning of this chapter, the missing element is **white-collar crime**. What exactly is meant by this term? According to Edwin Sutherland (whose book, *White-Collar Crime*, was first published in 1949), it is

> a crime committed by persons of respectability and high social status in the course of his [sic] occupation.[22]

The importance of Sutherland's work lay in the recognition that 'persons of the upper socio-economic class engage in much criminal behaviour'. This clearly refuted earlier theories of crime which saw poverty and personal pathology as the main causes of crime. As Sutherland remarked, it would be foolish to suggest that 'the crimes of the Ford Motor Company are due to the Oedipus complex'. (It would be equally foolish to suggest that corporate or employee offending could be attributed to poverty.) Such crimes are organised, deliberate and are motivated simply by money.

> ... the corporation comes closer to the 'economic man' and to 'pure reason' than any other person or any other organisation ... The corporation selects crimes which involve the smallest danger of detection and identification and against which the victims are least likely to fight ... The corporations attempt to prevent the implementation of the law and to create general goodwill.[23]

According to Sutherland, what distinguished rich from poor offenders were the procedures used to deal with offenders. He argued that while both groups committed crime, the higher social groups benefited from the differential implementation of the law. They did not suffer the stigma of formal criminalisation or the 'public resentment' which was orchestrated against 'traditional' criminals (at that time, primarily through the medium of the press).

Since 1949 the worlds of the media and commerce and business have changed beyond recognition. Nevertheless, the essence of Sutherland's definition is evident in recent work, notably that of Hazel Croall who has modified and widened it to produce

> a broad, inclusive definition in which white-collar crime is ... defined as the abuse of a legitimate occupational role which is regulated by law.[24]

Although the issue of social status is not uppermost here, the key element of white-collar crime – breaking the law while engaged in legitimate work – still remains. But it is important to recognise that crime committed at work may take very different forms: it may be committed for the benefit of the individual or for the benefit of the organisation. White-collar crime is therefore best seen as an 'umbrella' term which covers a wide spectrum of crimes *for* and crimes *against* business (see Figure 3.4).

Figure 3.4: **White-collar crime**

For business
- Corporate crime
- Fraud (organisational)

Against business
- Embezzlement
- Fraud (individual)
- Occupational crime ('fiddling' at work)

CRIMES AGAINST BUSINESS

Where crimes against business are concerned, offences can include embezzlement, computer fraud and a wide variety of 'occupational crimes'. The latter can range from theft from the workplace to fiddling expenses, although they are often perceived as 'perks' by those who commit them.[25] A survey conducted for the Confederation of British Industry (CBI) in 1990[26] found that only one employee in 12 considered stealing from work to be a crime. The CBI estimated that workplace crime was at that time costing around £5 billion a year. But any figure placed on the costs of such crimes is bound to be a 'guesstimate' because white-collar offences are so effectively hidden – they take place in the private arena of work, involve an entirely different level of secrecy from 'traditional' crimes and require very different methods of investigation.

FRAUD

These differences are well illustrated by the 1983 *Keith Committee Report* in its analysis of the problems involved in investigating tax fraud.

> In ordinary police work the police first learn that a crime has been committed from the victim or bystanders, and once a suspect has been identified, major evidential contributions come from witnesses or clues found at the scene of the crime. By contrast, in tax fraud

cases, the revenue agency itself is the unknowing victim ... The question for investigation is not 'who has done it?' but 'has anything been done?' and to establish ... [the existence of] fraud requires an initial investigation in circumstances where all or nearly all the evidence is likely to be in the hands of the suspect.[27]

As Figure 3.4 shows, fraud may be committed for or against the interests of the organisation or business. And so the *Keith Committee Report*'s question – 'has anything been done?' – is therefore supplemented by another equally difficult question: 'why, and for whom, did they do it?'. The answers given to both are often very confused – perhaps deliberately so. For example, in the recent Nat West Markets scandal we are told that it is 'unclear' whether the massive financial losses incurred (detailed below) arose as a result of 'personal gain or mis-judgement'.[28] In this way, the boundaries between acceptable business practice and crime are blurred: former MP Jonathan Aitken described this boundary (in his words, between 'a knighthood and the Old Bailey') as simply the difference between success and failure.

At the time of writing this chapter, the Bank of England and other international regulators are reported to be engaged in 'a high level effort to plug the holes in global banking supervision'.[29] This initiative comes in the wake of a series of banking scandals which, over the past two years, have included the following international groups:

- Sumitomo Corporation of Japan lost £1.6. billion on suspicious copper trades involving trader Yasuo Hamanaka (made public in June 1996);
- Barings of Britain lost £865 million on Japanese futures trades by Nick Leeson (made public in February 1995);
- Daiwa Bank of Japan lost £680 million over 11 years on US Treasury bond transactions involving trader Toshihide Iguchi (made public in September 1995);
- Deutsche Bank of Germany lost £438 million on the purchase of unregistered securities by one of its leading fund managers, Peter Young (made public in September 1996);
- Nat West Markets, the investment banking arm of National Westminster Bank, lost £89 million on mis-priced European interest-rate options contracts by trader Kyriacos Papouis (made public in February 1997).

Revelations of further £50 million losses at Nat West Markets have been blamed on the 'six and seven figure bonuses to City traders', which encouraged them to act 'recklessly'. According to City sources (which were widely reported in the media), this 'over enthusiastic trading' on the part of individuals is a reflection of 'the need to meet performance targets'. Such excuses are not easily applied to other forms of crime – it is unlikely that social security claimants who defraud the system by working on the side would be regarded as just 'over enthusiastic' in their efforts to make ends meet.

The very language associated with these huge financial frauds is managerial, low-key and not censorious – it reflects the view that such offences are merely a matter of pushing enterprise a little too far, rather than breaking the law. It seems that the pressure to **succeed** is regarded as an understandable justification for the crimes of the rich, but pressure to **survive** is regarded as insufficient to justify many crimes of poverty (see Chapters 4 and 5). At the same time, the existence of legislative 'grey areas' (particularly around taxation, business and commercial law) can create confusion over what precisely *is* a criminal act anyway! In this way, the 'letter of the law' may itself provide the scope to break or circumvent its spirit (see Chapter 4).

While the law may encourage aspiring entrepenurs to act 'recklessly' and 'push' the boundaries of the law still further, the outcome is almost beyond comprehension. The banking scandal losses of the last two years appear almost insignificant when compared to the £12 – £15 *billion* estimated to have been lost in the massive frauds uncovered in the Bank of Credit and Commerce International (BCCI) in 1991. The infamous BCCI was also referred to in the 'quality' press as the 'Bank of Crooks and Criminals International' and 'Bank of Cocaine, Conmen and Imposters'.[30] To put the seriousness and scale of fraud into perspective, it needs to be compared with the 'ordinary' crime which dominates the crime agenda.

> In police terms any crime involving more than a few thousand pounds is likely to be seen as 'serious'. Yet fraud occupies a different perceptual category, as if, once one passes a certain figure, the number of additional 'zeros' becomes irrelevant ... the costs of crime in England and Wales in 1990 totalled some £432 million for theft of and from vehicles, £800 million for burglary, and £500 million for arson. The alleged frauds in any one of the more serious cases – involving BCCI, Barlow Clowes, Guinness, Maxwell and

Polly Peck – approach or exceed these figures ... To illustrate this starkly, Robert Maxwell and others allegedly looted from pension funds alone a sum equal to the total financial losses from car crime.[31]

CORPORATE CRIME

The crimes of the rich are costly in terms of life and health as well as in terms of hard cash. This is best exemplified in the case of breaches of Health and Safety laws which lead to employee illness, injury and death. Using figures from the Health and Safety Executive (HSE) from 1983–88, Pearce and Tombs summarised the seriousness of violations of health and safety law by businesses and corporations:

> ... management have been cited as responsible for '2 out of 3' deaths in general manufacturing ... '3 out of 5' farm deaths ... 78 per cent of fatal maintenance accidents in manufacturing... 70 per cent of deaths in the construction industry, and so on. *In other words, in at least two out of three fatal accidents, managements were in violation of the Health and Safety at Work Act 1974 in terms of their general duties to employees.* Popular definitions of an 'accident' are called into question by such data.[32] (emphasis in original)

As long ago as 1983, Steven Box persuasively argued that if work-related deaths (due to injuries and avoidable occupational diseases) were compared to the homicide rate in Britain, the ratio of deaths would be 7 to 1.[33] If we take more recent HSE data it is probable that little has changed.

In 1995/96 the HSE recorded a total of 338 fatal injuries (compared with 376 in 1994/95). But it should be stressed that this figure does not include deaths due to the longer-term effects of work-related illness or injury, which would undoubtedly increase the total considerably. In the comparable year, 1995, the Home Office recorded 745 homicides. These 745 homicides occupied disproportionately more media space, political commentary and investigatory effort than that devoted to the 338 deaths at work. It is significant that the HSE inspectors who 'police' the safety of our workplaces numbered 1,424 in 1995/96, compared with over 127,000 police officers in England and Wales.[34]

The risks of accidents at work are concentrated in certain sectors of the economy: workers in the construction and farming industries have long had the highest 'injury rate'. But, in the early 1990s, channel tunnel workers suffered an injury rate (at 4.7 per cent) far higher than the overall rate (of 1.8 per cent) for construction workers as a whole. The economic push to construct the tunnel had profound costs in terms of workers' lives. The deaths were often placed in the context of the Chunnel project itself, which embodied the risks and challenges of 'cutting-edge' technology. This argument is reminiscent of the rationale given for deaths resulting from the extraction of North Sea Oil.[35]

In 1988 the North Sea Piper Alpha oil platform exploded with the loss of 167 lives – it was the world's worst oil disaster. The rig's then owners (Occidental) moved swiftly to compensate victims' families – the average award being £600,000 per fatality. No prosecution was mounted despite the fact that the subsequent Cullen Report was deeply critical of safety training and inspections (one of which occurred just a month before the disaster), which it described as 'cursory' and 'superficial'. At the time, North Sea Oil revenues were worth £3 billion a year to the Exchequer and the government department responsible for inspecting safety was the same department which had most to gain from speedy extraction of oil – the Department of Trade and Industry. As long ago as 1980 the Burgoyne Committee had recommended safety be the responsibility of a single *independent* agency, but the HSE did not assume responsibility for oil platform safety until a decade later, after the Cullen Report on the Piper Alpha disaster.

As a postscript, the successor platform to Piper Alpha, Piper Bravo, has recently been the subject of safety memos from the HSE regulators to owners Elf. The documentation (leaked to the press in March 1997), indicated that maintenance records for ventilation and fire-fighting equipment on the rig were incomplete. The concern expressed in Aberdeen was testimony to the sensitivity of the local community to safety issues and to their concerns that financial considerations may be influencing North Sea safety in this lucrative area of the economy.

SUMMARY: SOME ALTERNATIVE CRIME 'PROBLEMS'

I. WHO COMMITS CRIME?

It is clear from the discussion in this chapter that crime is committed by members of all social groups, by the rich and the poor, by individuals and complex organisations.

- Where **occupational crime** is concerned many would agree with Stuart Henry[36] that 'everyone, from dustman to doctors and from directors to dockers, is on the fiddle'.
- For the unemployed, work in the casualised **hidden economy** provides some opportunities for fiddling, though these are less lucrative and limited than full-time work.[37]
- For **business**, the 'culling' of a variety of regulations (under the political banner of cutting 'red tape') has freed them to self-regulate and to self-assess their own compliance to regulatory laws: as we will see in Chapters 4 and 6, this applies to both Inland Revenue and environmental laws, where scope for offending has clearly been increased.
- For the **trans-national corporation**, 'the sky is the limit' where the scope for law-breaking is concerned. As Levi noted,[38] we appear incredulous when faced with the vast the sums of money at stake in corporate fraud. We seem to be equally powerless to combat the threat to life and health which corporate violations of environmental, health and safety, and food and drug laws pose to the local, national and global community.[39]

2. WHO SUFFERS MOST AS A RESULT OF CRIME?

In terms of the political, popular and media concern, there is a 'vast difference between serious crimes and crimes taken seriously'.[40] What have been termed corporate crimes can be regarded as more serious (in terms of threat to life and health) and more costly than the 'traditional' crimes which dominate the current crime agenda. Although Chapter 6 will examine patterns of criminal victimisation in more detail, it is worth noting the range of victims who suffer as a result of white-collar crimes:

- victims of commercial fraud may be investors, pensioners, pension funds, competitors and entire banking systems;
- victims of price-fixing, trading violations, tax and VAT frauds may be consumers, legitimate businesses and taxpayers;
- victims of corporate crime may be employees, investors, competitors and all who depend on the integrity of global economic systems. In the case of pollution and safety violations, we are *all* potential victims of environmental disasters.

3. WHO GETS CAUGHT, AND WHO GOES TO COURT?

The earlier discussion of crime statistics raised a number of problems of reliability and interpretation. In summary, official figures of **recorded crime** only represent a partial picture of all crimes committed, and so the data consequently collected on **known offenders** is based on only a limited sample of those who have broken the law – in other words, on those who have been caught and found guilty. In the next chapter we will examine how and why certain individuals and groups are more likely to be caught, arrested, prosecuted and punished than others. The key themes which will emerge have been touched on in the comparison between traditional and white collar crime: they centre on issues of the **visibility** of the crime and the **knowledge and power** of the offender.

NOTES

1   R Matthews and J Young, *Re-Thinking Criminology: the realist debate*, Sage, 1992.

2   D Kidd-Hewitt and R Osborne (eds), *Crime and the Media: a post-modern spectacle*, Pluto Press, 1995.

3   Galtung and Ruge, 'Selecting and structuring news', in S Cohen and J Young (eds), *The Manufacture of News*, Constable, 1973; S Hall *et al*, *Policing the Crisis*, Macmillan, 1978.

4   M Bauer, 'Crime in the 1990s: a federal perspective', in *Federal Probation*, No 53, 1989, p36.

5   Home Office, *Criminal Statistics for England and Wales: 1995*, HMSO, 1996, p224.

6   *Ibid.*

7   M Fitzgerald and C Hale, *Ethnic Minorities: victimisation and racial harassment*, Home Office Research Study No 154, Home Office, 1996.

8   C Mirrlees-Black, P Mayhew and A Percy, *The 1996 British Crime Survey, England and Wales*, Home Office Statistical Bulletin 19/96, Home Office, 1996.

9   Fitzgerald and Hale, *see* note 7.

10 G Pearson, *Hooligan: a history of respectable fears*, Macmillan, 1983, p210.

11 N Dennis and G Erdos, *Families Without Fatherhood*, IEA Health and Welfare Unit, Choice in Welfare No 12, IEA, 1993, p83.

12 *Ibid.*

13 J Young and J Lea, *What's To Be Done About Law and Order?*, Pluto Press, 2nd edn, 1993.

14 M Keith, 'From punishment to discipline? Racism and the policing of social control' in M Keith and M Cross (eds), *Racism, the City and the*

State, Routledge, 1993.

15 Mirrlees-Black, Mayhew and Percy, *see* note 8.

16 M Hough and P Mayhew, *The British Crime Survey*, Home Office Research Study 76, HMSO, 1983.

17 *Ibid.*

18 Mirrlees-Black, Mayhew and Percy, *see* note 8.

19 Mirrlees-Black, Mayhew and Percy, *see* note 8, p30.

20 *Racially Motivated Crime*, 1994.

21 *Wolverhampton Crime Audit*, 1996.

22 W Sutherland, *White-Collar Crime*, Holt, Rinehart and Winston, 1949.

23 *Ibid.*

24 H Croall, *White-Collar Crime*, Open University Press, 1992.

25 G Mars, *Cheats at Work*, Allen & Unwin, 1984; D Cook, *Rich Law, Poor Law: different responses to tax and supplementary benefit fraud*, Open University Press, 1989.

26 Confederation of British Industry, 1990.

27 *Keith Committee Report on the Enforcement Powers of the Revenue Departments*, Cmnd 8822, HMSO, 1983, para 8.5.

28 *Guardian*, 1 March 1997.

29 *Guardian*, 31 March 1997.

30 Croall, *see* note 24, p29.

31 M Levi, 'Serious fraud in Britain: criminal justice versus regulation', in F Pearce and L Snider (eds), *Corporate Crime: contemporry debates*, University of Toronto Press, 1995, p184.

32 F Pearce and S Tombs, 'Ideology, hegemony and empiricism: compliance theories of regulation', in *British Journal of Criminology*, Vol 30, No 4, 1990.

33 S Box, *Power, Crime and Mystification*, Tavistock, 1983.

34 HSE, *Annual Report*, 1997; Home Office, *Digest 3: Information on the Criminal Justice System in England and Wales*, Home Office Research and Statistical Department, 1995.

35 W Carson, *The Other Price of Britain's Oil*, Martin Robertson, 1982.

36 S Henry, *The Hidden Economy*, Martin Robertson, 1978.

37 D Cook, *see* note 25; H Dean and M Melrose, 'Manageable discord: fraud and resistance in the social security system', in *Social Policy and Administration*, Vol 31, No 2, 1997.

38 Levi, *see* note 31.

39 U Beck, *Risk Society*, Sage, 1992; Croall, *see* note 24; J Braithwaite, *Corporate Crime in the Pharmaceutical Industry*, RKP, 1984.

40 B Hudson, *Penal Policy and Social Justice*, Macmillan, 1993, p77.

Robert Maxwell and others allegedly looted from pension funds alone the equivalent of the total financial losses from car crime.

Credit: The Guardian

4 Poverty, punishment and justice

INTRODUCTION

Justice is a two-way street – but criminal justice is a one-way street.
Individuals owe obligations to their fellow citizens because their
fellow citizens owe obligations to them. Criminal justice focuses on
the first and looks away from the second. (J Reiman, *The Rich Get
Richer and the Poor Get Prison*, Macmillan, New York, 1990, p124
(emphasis in original))

The title of Reiman's book, *The Rich Get Richer and the Poor Get
Prison*, conveys a central argument of this chapter, and an important
theme in this book. Reiman pointedly reminds us that it is impossible
to separate out issues of criminal and social justice – in a just society,
they should be part of the same 'two-way street'. This chapter will
look at the criminal justice process in order to assess if **justice** is
done, for the rich and the poor in contemporary British society.

First we will trace the differing ways in which (relatively rich)
white-collar offenders and (often poor) 'traditional' offenders are
filtered out of and into the formal criminal justice system. Secondly,
we will look at the sentencing process in the courts and at the
external factors which have, in recent years, shaped sentencing
practice. Many factors beyond the scope of the crime committed
and the offender being sentenced can influence the criminal justice
process. These include, for example, changes in the law; moral 'panics'
over certain crimes; horrific crimes (such as the Jamie Bulger murder
in 1993); and local and national pressure group campaigns.

While the seriousness of the offence is one key determinant, it is
essential to recognise the importance of the **offender-specific**

factors which also affect sentencing and punishment decisions. And so, thirdly, this chapter will analyse the ways in which issues of

- age
- gender
- 'race' and ethnicity
- economic status
- family and social indicators

are interpreted by criminal justice practitioners. Ultimately, the combined effects of external, offence and offender-related factors serve to filter the rich *out of*, and the poor *into*, prison.

Fourthly, we will move on to look at **who** gets punished and **why**. This begs a further series of crucial questions:

- What kinds of people currently fill our prisons – **who is the 'identikit prisoner**?
- *Why* do we send people to prison – prison **as** punishment or **for** punishment?
- Does punishment **reduce crime** and does prison *work*?
- Is there a link between **poverty, unemployment and imprisonment**?
- **Does crime and punishment pay**? The rewards of crime and the crime control industry.

WEALTH, POVERTY AND THE CRIMINAL JUSTICE PROCESS

As the discussion of white-collar crime in Chapter 3 has shown, these offences are by their nature extremely difficult to detect: the difficulty is as much one of establishing *if* a crime has been committed as establishing the identity of the offender. This is the starting point for very different approaches to the policing of white-collar and traditional crimes. In the case of the former, it is often accepted that most offenders will 'get away with it' and so the primary goal is to **regulate** offending and encourage **compliance** to the law. This is particularly clear in the case of tax evasion. As one tax official told me, 'the responsibility of the Revenue is to get money in and not to lock people up in prison'.[1] By the same token, there is official recognition that

Anyone who commits an elaborate fraud knows he will probably not be prosecuted and that, if prosecuted, it will take years to formulate charges and that he will probably escape the main charges.[2]

And if, and when, cases *do* come to trial,

> It is often difficult for a jury to understand what fraud cases are about. Often judges do not understand it themselves.[3]

One of the main reasons for the disparity in the treatment of white-collar and traditional crime is the **letter of the law**. In general, the laws governing business and commercial life are more complex than the laws governing individual behaviour. For example, in his study of corporate crime in the pharmaceutical industry, Braithwaite[4] argued that individual legal sanctions are 'reserved for specific harmful acts which occur at a specific point in time', but corporate crime usually arises from a 'harmful pattern of conduct'. This raises problems of exactly **who is responsible** for these patterns of conduct? Can a **chain of causation** be proven, which links those responsible with the harm itself? For instance, who is responsible for a dangerous drug reaching the public market – the laboratory technicians who may have falsified test results, their supervisors, the company's marketing department or board of directors who exerted pressure for commercial success, or anyone (and everyone) who possibly 'turned a blind eye' to illegalities?[5]

To give an everyday example of how the letter of the law can affect the process of justice, we can take the example of 'water pollution'. In law this is defined as:

> to cause or knowingly permit a noxious substance to enter a watercourse. (section 85 Water Resources Act, 1989)

To prove a case of water pollution, the Environmental Agency (previously National Rivers Authority) inspectors have to prove a *continuous* chain of liability for the incident – from the end of a factory pipe discharging into the water, to the evidence of the pollution which was **caused** directly by that substance. The evidence may be discoloured water, toxic substances in the watercourse or dead fish some distance downstream: on a lengthy stretch of canal or an estuary with several industrial 'dischargers' this level of proof is not easy to establish.[6] Once again, a criminal law primarily based on a concept of crime as a fixed incident, at a fixed time and place, is not appropriate for the type of offences which businesses commit. Neither does it facilitate effective prosecution of these offenders.

It is hardly surprising that those engaged with the task of regulating the conduct of commerce and business (whether regulating pharmaceutical companies, taxation, or pollution) often adopt compliance strategies. These stress negotiation, bargaining and formal warnings to secure compliance with the law: they usually reserve criminal prosecution for only the most serious cases.[7] As a result, **private justice** takes precedence over criminal justice for most white-collar offences.

Figure 4.1: **Issues shaping criminal justice decisions (for 'white-collar' and 'traditional' offenders)**

Sphere of decision making   **Decisive issues**

Policing and regulation

- Visibility of the crime
- Perceived seriousness of the crime
- The letter of the law (proof of intent or strict liability?)
- Access to evidence
- Extent of police/regulators' powers
- Policing/regulation strategy (compliance or prosecution policy?)
- Availability of investigatory resources

Prosecution and sentencing

- Crime seriousness
- Ability to 'pay' for crime (private justice?)
- Access to legal advice and representation
- Cautioning policy and practice
- Bail and remand decisions
- Corrigible or incorrigible offender? (referral for probation, psychiatric reports)
- Positive or negative economic, social and family indicators
- Previous convictions or previous 'good character'
- Judgements about the offender's 'threat' to society

Is private justice for corporate and business crime inevitably 'a bad thing'? Braithwaite[8] argues 'no', and puts forward an approach to regulation which includes the following four elements:

- taking crime seriously;
- nurturing dialogue as an alternative to the criminal process;
- empowering public interest groups as third parties in the regulation process;
- being flexible and seeing the contradictory effects of regulation (that the 'medicine' for today's case could be poison for tomorrow's).

In the case of his final point, other commentators would agree that penalties can have perverse effects. For instance, pursuing **corporate liability** through the courts may be counter-productive:

> Punishing the corporation alone might well induce it to clean up its act, but such punishment, almost always a fine, could be regarded as not much more than an unfortunate consequence – some bad luck – and written off as another cost of doing business.[9]

On the other hand, it could be argued that without ultimate corporate liability, justice cannot be done. But proving corporate liability means being able to blame the 'controlling mind' of the organisation. For example, in the tragic case of the Herald of Free Enterprise ferry disaster, the blame was located at a variety of levels, from individual to corporation – from the man who failed to close the bow doors, to the captain, to the board of directors. The failure of the corporate manslaughter case against P&O European Ferries left 192 victims dead and a 'crime without punishment'.[10]

Braithwaite's four-fold strategy offers one way forward to better police white-collar crimes. But for his approach to be effective, the agencies who regulate business must have a strong legal framework and a range of formal and informal sanctions they can use: in other words, to be effective regulators, they must be able to 'walk quietly, while holding a big stick'.[11] This brings us back to the letter of the law (which ultimately determines if that stick is 'big' enough to deter offending), and to the law-makers themselves.

Where law-making is concerned, it is important to recognise that law is not produced in a social, political and economic vacuum. For example, corporate and business representatives are often consulted by, and have powerful lobbies to influence, those politicians who define and draft the laws which regulate their activities.[12] By contrast, car thieves and burglars are not similarly consulted about the provisions of Criminal Justice Bills which may affect their business!

Where does the letter of the law leave the poorer offender? To take one example, if we compare the burden of proof which the law requires in cases of tax evasion with that required in social security fraud cases, the contrast is stark. The offences available to the Inland Revenue require proof of *dishonesty* or of **intent** to defraud. Social security fraud only needs proof that the offender *knowingly made a false statement* in claiming benefit – a matter of **strict liability**. And so it is very difficult to prove 'dishonesty' or intent to defraud taxes, but relatively easy to prove the falsity of a statement on a benefit claim. As Chapter 5 will argue, the letter of the law therefore encourages the criminalisation of the fiddling of the poor, but a compliance approach to the fiddling of the rich.

Where the policing and investigation of white-collar crime is concerned, the regulatory agencies involved are relatively under-resourced[13] (see Chapters 3 and 5). By contrast, public expenditure on the 43 police forces in England and Wales, which primarily deal with 'traditional' crime, was over £6 billion in 1993/94.[14] According to the Audit Commission, the annual cost of policing in 1994/95 amounted to an average of £101 per head of the population.[15]

As Figure 4.1 demonstrates, the decision to prosecute (or not) may also depend on an offender's **ability to pay** for their crime which, in turn, is largely a reflection of their class position. For instance, cases of criminal damage to restaurants or clubs may not proceed into the criminal justice system if the 'high spirited' (and high status) individuals involved can afford to pay for the damage done. Similarly, those who can repay taxes defrauded (with appropriate interest) effectively receive private justice, whereas benefit fraudsters are more likely to pay twice – through repayment of benefits overpaid to them, and possibly criminal prosecution too.[16]

Another decisive issue in shaping criminal justice is the defendant's access to **legal advice and representation**. Clearly, better-off offenders are more likely to have knowledge of and access to the best lawyers (and accountants). Poorer defendants are more likely to depend on legal aid and, in police stations and magistrates' courts, on the duty solicitor scheme. There has been an explosion in the costs of legal aid over the past decade, both in terms of numbers of cases where assistance was granted and in the costs incurred. Expenditure on legal aid rocketed from £306 million in 1985 to £1.4 billion in 1995.[17] But legal aid 'inflation' has been due to a number of factors:

• **changes in prosecution policies:** as the state takes legal action, so defendants have to defend themselves;

- **increases in the complexity and volume of laws:** for example, the *three* major Criminal Justice Acts in the years 1991–94;
- **knock-on effects of government policies:** for example the Police and Criminal Evidence Acts (PACE, 1984 and 1994) which involved the delivery of legal aid services to those detained by police (PACE created more demand for services, of greater complexity);
- **increasing poverty and unemployment:** 85 per cent of applicants for criminal legal aid are unemployed. If current trends continue, demand will grow (see Chapter 2).[18]

The reforms of the legal aid system announced by the Lord Chancellor in July 1996 will mean a further 'rationing' of services which are already over-stretched. As David Wall argues, this will have a profound effect on the legitimacy of the criminal justice system:

> … the most realistic expectation that we can currently have of legal aid is that it can be used to 'ameliorate injustice in the criminal justice process itself', thus providing a low level of protection for the individual and also a degree of legitimacy to the actions of state organisations. The main problem we currently face is that the proposals to control the delivery of legally aided criminal services threaten even these minimal functions of legal aid and threaten to throw criminal justice into a greater legitimation crisis than that which already exists … surely the £350 million or so pounds we pay for criminal legal aid is still a relatively cheap price to pay for that legitimacy.[19]

A very cheap price to pay, to keep open just one lane of the 'two-way street' between criminal and social justice.

EXTERNAL FACTORS SHAPING CRIMINAL JUSTICE

The discussion of legal aid has already demonstrated the impact of government policies on the operation of criminal justice. The Home Office is obviously aware of the knock-on effects of legislative change, media campaigns and high profile crime cases on the criminal justice process – in their latest statistics they included an analysis of trends in imprisonment which specifically noted these external factors (see Figure 4.2).

Most notably, Figure 4.2 shows that the legislative changes of the Criminal Justice Acts of 1991, 1993 and the Criminal Justice and Public Order Act of 1994 have all been accompanied by a dramatic rise in the use of imprisonment. The 1991 Act, implemented in October 1992, had firmly connected sentencing with the seriousness of the crime, and so confirmed that custody should generally be reserved for the *most serious* offences.[20] At the same time, we should not underestimate the impact of the murder of Jamie Bulger in February 1993 on 'law and order' anxieties in general, and on concerns about youth crime in particular: both sets of concerns were reflected in the provisions of the 1993 Act.

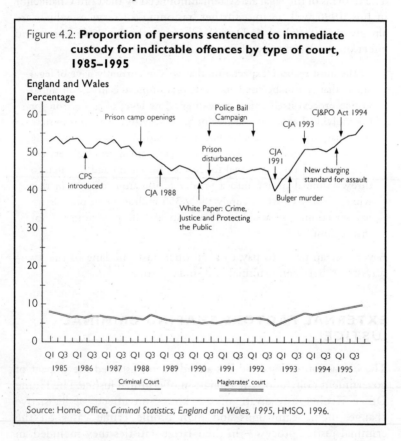

Figure 4.2: **Proportion of persons sentenced to immediate custody for indictable offences by type of court, 1985–1995**

Source: Home Office, *Criminal Statistics, England and Wales, 1995*, HMSO, 1996.

The use of prison for remands in custody was also accentuated by the police campaign against 'bail bandits' (defendants who, it was said, committed a significant number of crimes while released on bail). But, at a very practical level, the impact of the prison building programme of the later 1980s also underpins the dramatic rise in the use of imprisonment in the 1990s: as Steven Box remarked, if we insist on building prisons, we can be certain that the judiciary and magistracy will fill them.[21]

Who will they fill the prisons with? It is not necessary to believe in a 'conspiracy theory' to understand how magistrates and judges imprison disproportionate numbers of poor, young, unemployed, non-white, males. As the latter part of this chapter will go on to discuss, there is an underlying belief among predominantly middle-class judges and magistrates that the poor (rather than the rich) pose a criminal and moral threat to law-abiding society.[22] Logically, such assumptions are bound to shape their sentencing practice, particularly in times of social and economic crisis when the 'threat' appears greatest.

OFFENDER-RELATED FACTORS SHAPING CRIMINAL JUSTICE

> By and large, the criminal law is imposed by whites on blacks; by the advantaged on the disadvantaged; by the elderly on the young and by men on women.[23]

Those who make the law, implement it and administer punishment are overwhelmingly male, white, middle-aged and middle class. It is therefore not surprising that an individual's age, gender, 'race' and class all impinge upon the way they are likely to be perceived by criminal justice professionals.

If we first address the issue of race, an important academic study of sentencing in four West Midlands Crown Courts concluded that, after offence-related variables were accounted for, there was a significant **'race effect'** in the sentencing of Black★ offenders.[24] And so, for example, in Dudley, Black offenders in the Crown Court had a 23 per cent higher chance of receiving a custodial sentence than their white counterparts, and at Warwick and Stafford Black people were also much more likely to receive a prison sentence.

The 'race effect' can best be seen as the product of several different factors operating at different stages of the criminal justice

---

★ See note on use of 'Black', p15.

process which, taken together, filter more Black people into, and fewer out of, the system. Lord Taylor described the compounding effects of a variety of decisions.

> A multiplier effect could operate, amplifying discrimination at several points. If a group was more likely to be stopped in the street and less likely to be cautioned, the effect was compounded. If the same group was less likely to be bailed and more likely to be tried at the crown court than the magistrates court, the effect could produce startling discrepancies.[25]

To understand this multiplier effect, it is necessary to unpack some of the issues raised here. If we start with policing, there is the tendency to target poorer areas (often with high minority ethnic populations) as crime prone (see also Chapter 1). As we have already seen (in Chapter 3), police targeting may produce a 'self-fulfilling prophecy' in terms of crimes discovered. The disproportionate use of police stop and search powers with young Black men similarly generates not only potential hostility, but also potential arrests.[26] The fact that fewer Black young people are cautioned may well arise because a caution involves an admission of guilt (which may be hotly contested). More arrests followed by fewer guilty pleas in court (which may have encouraged more lenient sentencing) accentuate the multiplier effect. More 'not-guilty' pleas can effectively push Black defendants towards the Crown Court, and the higher sentences which may be imposed there. In addition, the tendency for the Crown Prosecution Service (prior to 1986, the police) to decide to opt for higher tariff offences for many Black defendants can also push them towards custodial sentences.[27] Finally, significantly higher proportions of Black (African–Caribbean – 42 per cent) and Asian (43 per cent) offenders were sentenced without the preparation of a Social Inquiry Report (now called a Pre-Sentence Report) for the court's information. This may be a reflection of the stereotypical view that minority ethnic offenders are more 'hardened' (incorrigible) than their white couterparts, and so less likely to respond positively to alternatives to custody.[28]

In their recent review of research on *Race and Criminal Justice*, the Penal Affairs Consortium[29] supports the conclusion of Marian Fitzgerald that

> there are ethnic differences in outcomes which can only be explained in terms of discrimination.[30]

This racial discrimination does not affect only the poor. But, as argued earlier, it is poorer localities which are disproportionately policed, and minority ethnic groups are disproportionately likely to live in these areas because they are more likely to suffer from the unemployment, low pay and diminished social security rights which cause poverty.[31] Consequently, the injustices of the criminal justice system compound the inequalities of wider society. For Black subjects there is, therefore, a clear relationship between **poverty, 'race' and punishment**, which is independent of any alleged link between poverty and the commission of crime itself.

Where issues of gender are concerned, Hudson argues that

> Poverty seems to be the key factor in the penal treatment of all women, as well as being the key precipitating factor in their criminality.[32]

Although women are 'on the whole, a law-abiding lot', most women's crimes are typically crimes of poverty – mainly relating to theft, handling stolen goods, drugs and prostitution.[33] Although they account for just over half of the British population, women accounted for only 18 per cent of 'known offenders' – those found guilty or cautioned – in 1995 (see Figure 4.3).

Although the number of known offences committed by women has increased over the past decade, their involvement in crime is still disproportionately low and their crimes less serious than their male counterparts. This may be due partly to the effectiveness of a variety of social controls over the lives of most women, who simply do not have the same opportunities as men for committing crime. For example, domestic reponsibilities are constraining:

> ... burglary is rendered more difficult when one is encumbered with a twin baby-buggy and its contents; constant care of a demented geriatric is not a conducive situation in which to plan a bank robbery.[34]

Despite such constraints, recent media panics have begun to focus on the allegedly increasing threat of female violent crime. For example, the BBC Panorama programme, *Violent Women*, screened in November 1996 was typically sensationalist. It highlighted the 'Jekyll and Hyde' women who allegedly become violent as a result of premenstrual syndrome, and argued that 'hundreds of thousands of men in Britain today' are being battered by their female partners. It is noteworthy that even press coverage echoed the 'shock, horror' tone of the programmes message – that women *could* be violent too. The *Guardian* headline covering this story (accompanied by a shaky photograph from video footage) read, 'This woman hits her husband'. Sadly, it is inconceivable that a parallel headline, 'This man hits his wife', would be regarded as shocking enough to warrant such a media exposé.

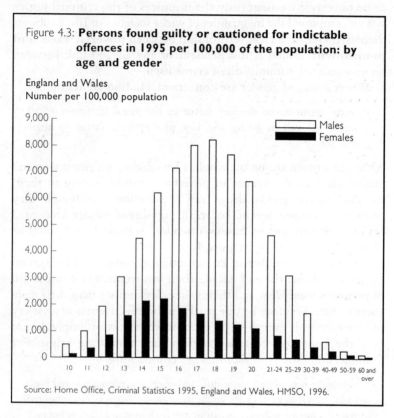

Figure 4.3: **Persons found guilty or cautioned for indictable offences in 1995 per 100,000 of the population: by age and gender**

England and Wales
Number per 100,000 population

Source: Home Office, Criminal Statistics 1995, England and Wales, HMSO, 1996.

Relating female violence to 'women's liberation', a clinical psychologist went on to predict that:

> It is possible that women could become as violent as men ... in the same way that they have become as sexually promiscuous and demanding as men, as keen on drinking alcohol, as keen on directing their agression outwards in all sorts of ways, in the workplace, in their relationships with men. There's a huge change taking place in the behaviour of women in every area and we're seeing it in the area of violence.[35]

But the women interviewed in the programme to illustrate this view were clearly not 'liberated'. (Like most known female offenders, they were young, disadvantaged, poor and powerless.) Nevertheless, accounts like these ultimately serve to keep women in their 'proper place' by reinforcing traditional roles – the shocking alternative is that, heaven forbid, women will bahave as badly as men!

The issues of gender, crime and justice produce several paradoxes. The first is that because women commit so little crime, those who do break the law and arrive in court, are often regarded as exceptional. One way to counter this exceptional status is to **play the gender game**.[36] If they are willing and able to explain their offending in ways which reinforce the traditional female stereotype (of feminity, domesticity and motherhood), they may attract less severe penalties in court. As a result, women who argue that they broke the law because of PMS, mental or physical illness will be seen as 'sad or mad rather than bad', and so their offending is **'rendered harmless'**.[37]

A second paradox is, as one solicitor admitted to Anne Worrall, that as far as many 'sick' women defendants are concerned,

> It isn't a doctor they need, it's a cheque book.[38]

But to admit this would be to challenge professional accounts of female offending. The gender game is a difficult and dangerous one to play.

Thirdly, any apparent success, in terms of 'lenient' sentences, can still lead to longer-term disadvantages. For example, a poorer woman who has committed a property crime and is portrayed as in need of 'help' may be offered a probation order. But if (because of her continued poverty) she re-offends, it is likely that she will be pushed up the punishment tarriff, and towards prison, much more quickly than her male counterpart. In this way, female offenders who play the gender game can be set up to fail. One result of this **ratchet effect** on sentencing is that women end up in prison for less serious offences and with fewer previous convictions than their male counterparts.[39]

Fourthly, some women cannot, or will not, play the gender game: they may be lone mothers on welfare, lesbians, have children in care or be involved in prostitution. Consequently, they may suffer from being seen as **doubly deviant** – in terms of their rejection of traditional gender roles, and because they have committed a crime.[40]

Where women in the criminal justice system are concerned, the treatment and punishment they receive is largely determined by how they are seen *as women*. In Carlen's words, female offenders are not portrayed as 'real' women – they are seen as 'either mad, masculine, menopausal or maladjusted'.[41] The 'justice' they receive is more to do with **who** they are than **what** they have done.

Issues of gender, race and social class all intersect at the point of judgements about an offender's family circumstances. As argued in Chapter 1, the family is often seen at the core of social problems and crime problems. In her study of 'social information' and its use in juvenile courts, Sheila Brown looked at the specific indicators used by magistrates to assess the defendants before them. She described magistrates' searches for relevant social information as inextricably bound up with what they saw as the 'pathology of offending'. Magistrates viewed family stability as the precondition for the moral and social order. This is reflected in the clusters of positive and negative indicators which inform their decision making.

Factors commonly taken as **negative indicators** (that is, bad influences) by magistrates included:

- the presence of offenders in the immediate or extended family;
- the 'single parent';
- an 'over protective' or 'immoral mother' ;
- alcoholism;
- problems in relationships with step-parents;
- parents not knowing the whereabouts of their offspring;
- parents' inability to get their children to school;
- working mothers, particularly where involved in evening work such as bar work;
- a home not deemed to be 'well kept';
- financial irresponsibility (eg, an over-preponderance of HP agreements);
- unwillingness or inability to punish children for their transgressions, particularly through deprivation of liberty (curfews) or financial penalties (stopping pocket money);
- a lack of appropriate concern about offending behaviour by parents.

Conversely, **positive indicators** (and good influences) were:

- 'natural' parents in a long-standing marriage;
- a husband in work with a full-time housewife;
- strong involvement between father and son, especially involving mutual leisure activities such as fishing or football;
- a 'well regulated' household (ie, demonstrating 'good standards' of housewifery/domesticity – 'does she keep a nice home?');

- parents maintaining contact with school;
- a strong manifestation of concern on the part of parents, especially willingness to co-operate with agencies and the courts to actively assist the court in applying sanctions.[42]

Very clear assumptions about the 'rightness' of the middle-class nuclear family frame these indicators. Crime is seen to be produced by the antithesis of this 'good family'. The impact on criminal justice is profound:

> This is an 'image of the working class family at its worst: central concepts are invoked of disorder and lack of moral fibre. The extensiveness of this image amongst the social control vocabulary of justices cannot be over-stressed.[43]

WHO GETS PUNISHED AND WHY?

Efforts to combat the race, class and gender biases of the criminal justice system seem to have had little impact. For instance, the anti-racism training given to police officers and sentencers has not, so far, removed the systematic discrimination within the system.[44] Moreover, it is still possible, in 1997, for a judge who uses the phrase 'work like niggers' in a Crown Court to continue in his post, and to suffer only a rebuke from the Lord Chancellor (who asked him to 'make a greater effort to guard against giving offence in future).[45]

Moves towards more equitable sentencing, attempted through the unit fine system, similarly failed. The system was introduced to enable magistrates to determine financial penalties in accordance with the *gravity* of offence (in units of seriousness) and the offender's *disposable income*. Unit fines, introduced in October 1992, were abolished only a year later when the 1993 Criminal Justice Act came into force. According to the Home Office,[46] the average fine for unemployed offenders fell from £90 to under £70 when unit fines were introduced, but climbed to £80 when the scheme was abolished. The corresponding changes for employed offenders were an increase from £140 to over £230 under unit fines, and a falling back to £160 when the scheme was abolished.

The fine accounted for 51 per cent of all sentences for indictable offences in magistrates' courts in 1989 but, by 1995, this had fallen to 37 per cent.[47] But if we look at sentences for *all offences* – including summary and motoring offences – the fine represented

75 per cent of all sentences passed in 1995.[48] This has a particular impact on poorer offenders who are least able to pay for their crimes through financial penalties. Significantly, three quarters of those who were imprisoned for fine default in 1994 were unemployed and in receipt of benefit.[49]

Prison can be seen as the hard end, and the end-point, of the criminal justice process. Figure 4.4 shows the pattern of flows through that process in 1995, demonstrating that of the 60,000 people sentenced to custody in that year, one-third were sentenced by magistrates and two-thirds by judges at Crown Courts. As the most serious offences are committed to trial at Crown Courts this is not entirely surprising. Leaving the issue of disparity in Crown Court sentencing to one side, other important issues arise concerning the one third of prisoners sentenced to custody by magistrates and the ability of the lay magistracy to ensure fairness and consistency in their practice.

At this stage, it is worth recapping a little of what is known about sentencing disparities between magistrates' courts in England and Wales. These disparities clearly influence *who* is sent to prison. Recent research by the National Association of Probation Officers (NAPO)[50] shows that a convicted person is:

- seven times more likely to be imprisoned in Chesterfield than in Wakefield;
- four times more likely to receive probation in Huddersfield than at Bow Street Magistrates' Court in London.

Clear inequities are also evident where custodial sentences for particular offences are compared. For instance, of those convicted of theft:

- 0.7 per cent were imprisoned in Swindon;
- 20.8 per cent in Hull;
- 24.5 per cent in Sunderland;
- and 37.3 per cent in Clerkenwell.

In order to answer the question '**who gets punished and why**' we perhaps need to beg more fundamental questions of the criminal justice system as a whole. Rather than seeing it as a means of controlling crime and dispensing justice, we could, alternatively, see it as a '**a system for sifting and classifying harms**'.[51] If the criminal justice system is seen in this way, then it fails to do so equitably on two counts:

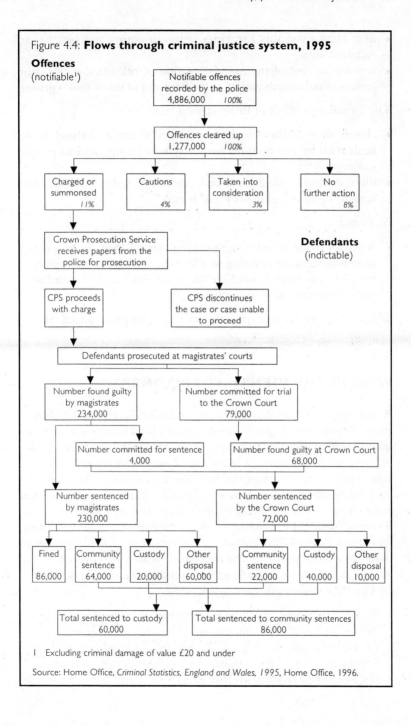

Figure 4.4: **Flows through criminal justice system, 1995**

Offences
(notifiable[1])

Notifiable offences
recorded by the police
4,886,000   *100%*

Offences cleared up
1,277,000   *100%*

| Charged or summonsed *11%* | Cautions *4%* | Taken into consideration *3%* | No further action *8%* |

Crown Prosecution Service
receives papers from the
police for prosecution

Defendants
(indictable)

CPS proceeds
with charge

CPS discontinues
the case or case unable
to proceed

Defendants prosecuted at magistrates' courts

Number found guilty
by magistrates
234,000

Number committed for trial
to the Crown Court
79,000

Number committed for sentence
4,000

Number found guilty at Crown Court
68,000

Number sentenced
by magistrates
230,000

Number sentenced
by the Crown Court
72,000

| Fined 86,000 | Community sentence 64,000 | Custody 20,000 | Other disposal 60,000 | Community sentence 22,000 | Custody 40,000 | Other disposal 10,000 |

Total sentenced to custody
60,000

Total sentenced to community sentences
86,000

1   Excluding criminal damage of value £20 and under

Source: Home Office, *Criminal Statistics, England and Wales, 1995*, Home Office, 1996.

- first, because of the disparities between courts and benches in different areas;
- second, because of the homogenisation of offenders, as the same groups of individuals end up at the hard end of the system – prison.

The cumulative effect of this system is to:

- classify those harms which are regarded as serious enough to be dealt with by the criminal justice system (as opposed to private justice);
- filter in those (often poor and powerless) individual offenders seen to be responsible for those harms.

As a result:

> When we arrive at the last stage, the prison population, we have the most homogeneous grouping in which the vast majority are poor, unskilled, uneducated, and have had much more contact with the criminal (and juvenile) justice systems.[52]

This brings us to consider the crucial questions posed at the beginning of this chapter.

WHO IS THE IDENTIKIT PRISONER?

As we have seen from data on known offenders (in Figure 4.3 above), those persons found guilty or cautioned for indictable offences are overwhelmingly young and male. As Sheldon indicates, they are also likely to be poor, have few educational qualifications and have had some earlier experience of the juvenile justice system. Accurate and up-to-date information on the social profile of those in custody is not currently available on any systematic basis. But in 1991 the Prison Reform Trust (PRT) produced a paper entitled *The Identikit Prisoner* which summarised information from a variety of available sources to build up a social profile of the individuals who then filled our penal establishments. Its main findings are reproduced in Figure 4.5.

The PRT discussion concluded:

> Taken as a whole, the 'Identikit Prisoner' is someone who has suffered a range of social and economic disadvantages. A key argument for reducing the use of prison is that, all too often, a period of imprisonment exacerbates those very disadvantages which have led the person into crime in the first place.[53]

Figure 4.5: **The Identikit Prisoner: 1991**

- 12 per cent of convicted prisoners and 17 per cent of remand prisoners were *homeless* at the time of their imprisonment

- 44 per cent of unconvicted prisoners and 31 per cent of convicted prisoners were *unemployed* prior to their imprisonment

- Over 40 per cent of prisoners have *no formal educational qualifications* on entering prison

- Around one third of prisoners suffer from some form of *psychiatric disorder* (according to an Institute of Psychiatry study of over 2,000 sentenced prisoners conducted by Professor John Gunn)

- *Drug abuse or dependency* affected 10 per cent of adult males and 24 per cent of female prisoners in the Gunn study

- 32 per cent of male prisoners and 47 per cent of female prisoners had *dependent children* living with them immediately prior to imprisonment

- Of those with dependent children, 91 per cent of male prisoners said partners or ex-wives were caring for them, compared with only 23 per cent of female prisoners (52 per cent of women prisoners said relatives were caring for their children, and 12 per cent were in care)

- Asked if they had experience of *local authority care* before the age of 16, 23 per cent of adult prisoners and 38 per cent of young prisoners replied they had

- 35 per cent of convicted prisoners said that someone in the *family* had also served a prison sentence

- 40 per cent of the prison population was *under 25* years, nearly two thirds were under 30.

- *Women* constituted just under 4 per cent of the prison population

- 16 per cent of the prison population was from *ethnic minority groups* (15.5 per cent of males and 26 per cent of females in 1990)

- Adult male prisoners of 'African or Afro-Caribbean origin' were serving sentences 44 per cent longer than those of adult white prisoners

Source: *The Identikit Prisoner*, Prison Reform Trust, 1991.

If, so far as possible, we update the findings of this survey, the results are depressing. In 1995 a total of 125,654 people were received in prison, either on remand, under sentence or as non-criminal prisoners (including fine defaulters and Immigration Act prisoners). As Table 4.1 indicates, the prison population reached an average of 51,00 in 1995, the highest level ever. Over 22 per cent of those prisoners were not convicted, but remanded in custody. If unconvicted prisoners are less likely to have homes and jobs at the time of their trial, then decisions about bail are effectively being determined by negative social circumstances rather than by 'justice' or the merits of the individual case. More generally, 'identikit prisoners' often suffer a combination of disadvantages (of class, gender, 'race', health, education and unemployment) which have a multiplier effect on their risks of imprisonment.

TABLE 4.1: **Prison population statistics: annual averages 1993–95**

	1993	1994	1995
Remand	10,700	12,400	11,400
Sentenced	33,300	35,800	39,100
Non-criminal prisoners	600	600	600
Total	**44,600**	**48,800**	**51,100**
Males	43,000	47,000	49,100
Females	1,600	1,800	2,000

Source: Home Office Research and Statistics Directorate, 1997

The prevalence of mental disorders among prisoners was recently the subject of two *British Medical Journal* articles.[54] The first concluded that 55 per cent of the sample of unconvicted prisoners surveyed had an 'immediate treatment need'. A second study, of Durham's remand prisoners, found that 26 per cent had one or more current mental disorders. Self-inflicted deaths in prisons numbered 47 in 1993; 62 in 1994; 60 in 1995; and 64 in 1996.[55]

On the issue of ethnicity, figures for 30 June 1995 show that 17 per cent of the male prison population and 24 per cent of the female population were known to be of ethnic minority origin (compared with 5.7 per cent of the overall population in Britain).[56] Of the 649 non-criminal prisoners held on 30 June 1995, 488 were Immigration Act prisoners (see Chapter 7 for a fuller discussion of immigration policy and criminalisation). Numbers of women imprisoned have increased, though their proportion of the average prison population in 1995 remains similar to that reported in the 1991 survey.

Research on users of bed and breakfast (B&B) accommodation, hostels, day centres and soup runs shows that the majority of users had been in custody in the last five years: the vicious circle of homelessness, offending, arrest, custodial remand and sentence is well demonstrated.[57] In 1995, homelessness charities claimed that

17,000 people were living in B&B in London – more than six times the official figure.[58] For ex-prisoners, their plight will be worsened by recent housing benefit changes which from April 1995 limited housing benefit to 13 weeks of absence from the property: those serving sentences of more than 13 weeks are therefore likely to lose their homes. (Under previous regulations, housing benefit could fully meet the rent payments of those serving up to a year in custody.)[59] The chances of these identikit prisoners 'going straight' under such circumstances are surely very slim.

Finally, we need to examine the extent of the threat these identikit prisoners pose to society. If we look at the sentenced population in 1995, 48 per cent were imprisoned for crimes of violence, sexual offences and robbery. But, if we include non-criminal prisoners and those on remand (22 per cent), the picture changes: in short, 63 per cent of prisoners in 1995 were *not* convicted of crimes involving violence, sex or robbery (having largely committed crimes against property). This begs questions about what precisely we send people to prison for.

WHAT IS PRISON FOR?

Reiman[60] argued it would be difficult to design a system to better 'maintain and encourage the existence of a stable and visible "class of criminals"' than the American criminal justice system – a system which British politicians are increasingly seeking to emulate. One way of looking at criminal justice policy is in terms of his 'pyrrhic defeat theory', whereby

> the failure of the criminal justice system yields such benefits to those in positions of power that it amounts to success.[61]

The failure to protect people from crime, failure to define the dangerous and costly offences of the rich as 'crime', failure to pursue the law equally vigorously against rich and poor alike all combine to

> create an image that crime is almost exclusively the work of the poor which serves the interests of the powerful.[62]

Reiman does not maintain that this is an intentional policy, but a more complex legacy and product of historical, legal and social conditions. At the same time he stresses that individuals are not entirely blameless for their criminal acts – in a useful analogy he argues that, after all, 'it would be foolhardy to refuse to fight a fire because its causes were suspect'. In addition (as the next chapter will show), so many victims of the crimes of the poor are the poor themselves.

But, one function of imprisonment can be seen as its ideological role in confirming **who 'real' criminals are**. A second, and more officially recognised one, is to deter and punish offenders, thereby reducing crime.

DOES PUNISHMENT REDUCE CRIME – DOES PRISON WORK?

As we have already seen in the discussion of the identikit prisoner, the effects of imprisonment work directly against 'going straight' and rates of recidivism bear out prison's failure. This is backed up by Home Office studies of 'criminal careers' which indicate that 60 per cent of all court appearances by males below the age of 40 years were attributed to 7 per cent of the male population – for them, clearly deterrence did *not work*. More generally, 56 per cent of male and 40 per cent of female prisoners were reconvicted within two years. Recidivism is particularly notable amongst younger offenders: two thirds of offenders aged under 21 were reconvicted within two years.[63]

Another key issue is whether we send people to prison *as* or *for* punishment. The classic justification of the prison is in terms of 'doing time' – in other words, punishment is **deprivation of liberty**, for a specified time, in accordance with the severity of the offence and culpability of the offender. The principle of less eligibility adds another dimension: it means that life 'inside' should be less comfortable than life for the poorest groups 'outside' the prison.[64] This argument – that the experience of imprisonment should be a punishment in itself – is frequently invoked in tabloid stories of 'easy-going' prison regimes. But the notion of prison as a holiday camp has recently taken on new meaning: in an effort to cope with the growing penal crisis, prison officials are

hoping to transform a former Pontins holiday camp near Morecambe, into a make-shift prison.[65]

On 28 February 1997 the prison population stood at an all-time high of 58,802 and was rising at the rate of around 220 per week.[66] Plans to use a 'floating jail' – the *HMP Weare* – moored off the Dorset coast initially appeared to have been scuppered when local residents opposed planning permission in January 1997. More recently, doubts have been expressed about the health and safety implications of taking in prisoners while structural alterations to the vessel were still taking place: the vessel is five storeys (30 metres) high with a capacity of 500, but inevitably the accommodation is claustrophobic, sealed, and partially below water level.[67] Despite these protests and reservations, the Weare is expected to receive its first intake of prisoners in June or July 1997. The cost of the facility and its transportation (from New York) was £5 million.[68]

The notion of 'warehousing' prisoners takes on an added dimension where other aspects of the current prison 'coping strategy' are concerned: the prison service has recently acquired ten 'Ready-to-Use (RTU) Units', formerly deployed to house Norwegian off-shore workers. (This accommodation is of good standard, although, perhaps understandably, the saunas have been removed.) A further seven RTUs are being purpose built to provide, in total, 680 additional prison places.[69]

Given the nature and extent of the current penal crisis, we perhaps need to pose some radically different questions about what we expect prisons to do. Alternative questions about the effectiveness of prisons could well question the 'liberal myth that we all want prisons to be better places'. Pat Carlen[70] focuses instead on '**prison's overwhelming power to punish**'. Some of the key questions she raises are:

- How successful are prisons in returning prisoners to society in a worse state of physical and mental health than they were in prior to imprisonment? How is this success achieved?
- How successful are prisons in engendering extremes of tension, fear and mental anguish in prisoners? How is this achieved?
- How successful are prisons in making the most of *any* pains already suffered by prisoners prior to their sentence?
- If people go to prison *as* punishment and not for punishment why are prisons not more like three star hotels? (emphasis in original)

Given earlier accounts of the vicious circle of imprisonment for the homeless, the mentally ill, the disadvantaged unemployed and poor, these are very serious questions indeed. But, at the same time, it is important to recognise the crucial symbolic function which prison fulfils.

Symbolically, prison demarcates between those behaviours society collectively condemns as being the worst imaginable and those it permits with varying degrees of tolerance. In doing this, the prison clarifies, maintains and reinforces the moral boundaries of society. It is difficult to imagine any other institution performing this function so well and effectively.[71]

POVERTY, UNEMPLOYMENT AND IMPRISONMENT – MANAGING PROBLEM POPULATIONS

The criminal justice system, and imprisonment in particular, also performs an important function in solving the problem of the 'human debris' produced by (post) industrial societies. In has not only a **symbolic** but a **physical** function in dealing with these 'unproductive elements'.[72] This was well described by Steven Box:

> These 'problem populations', unrequired by the productive process but actually or symbolically threatening it, become perceived as a nuisance eligible for state intervention. If they are 'social junk' … such as the mentally ill, old, sick or disabled, they have to be *managed*; if they are 'social dynamite', such as the unemployed or the unemployable, they have to be *controlled*.[73] (emphasis in original)

Prisons are, therefore, seen to defuse and deter any threats to the social order posed by potentially 'social dynamite' groups – those with least investment in society, fewest bonds to the social order and 'nothing to lose'. These groups are predominantly the young, male, (disproportionately) Black, unemployed and also those women who fail to adhere to traditional feminine and domestic norms. Unsurprisingly perhaps, these constitute the 'identikit' criminal and prisoner in contemporary Britain.

The management of problem populations is achieved through stereotypes of the 'common criminal' as well as through the penal process itself, because these images shape the ways in which criminal justice professionals act and react.

> The behaviour of the police, probation officers and magistrates and judges brings about the imprisonment of more unemployed and economically marginalised people not because the government demands it, but because each of these groups has its own rationale for regarding the unemployed with more suspicion and caution.[74]

To recap on the argument presented in Chapter 2, while evidence of a causal relationship between poverty and crime remains equivocal, there is a clearer relationship between poverty and punishment.[75] In times of economic crisis the rate of imprisonment increases because

> In periods of economic decline a discursive chain of punitiveness and severity spreads across our society.[76]

A crucial link in this discursive chain is the powerful image which equates the poor (and poverty itself) with crime.

DOES CRIME AND PUNISHMENT PAY?

Finally, it is essential to explore some of the economic reasons for the continued and expanding use of prison, as the end point of the criminal justice system. According to former Home Secretary Michael Howard, 'prison works' (although all evidence presented here points to the contrary), and this is one of the primary rationales underlying the privatisation and expansion of prisons over the past decade. Another rationale might be that even if 'crime does not pay', punishment clearly does.

Nils Christie powerfully argues that crime control is an industry, with an endless supply of 'raw material' and which 'provides profit and work while at the same time producing control of those who otherwise might have disturbed the social process'.[77] The penetration of criminal justice (along with most local and national agencies) by management ideology has produced an emphasis on efficiency, results and cost-effectiveness. Like higher education and the health service, criminal justice is now run as a business.

But the business analogy falters if we examine the relative cost-effectiveness of penal measures (Figure 4.6).

If cost-effectiveness was a key indicator, if rates of recidivism were a performance measure, if the quality of the 'customer's' experience was quantified, the business of criminal justice in England and Wales would surely be bankrupt. If the USA is an exemplar of what is to come, profits are guaranteed, but social order is not. As Vivien Stern, formerly Director of the National Association for the Care and Resettlement of Offenders (NACRO), reminds us,

> In 1994, one out of every three black men in the US between the ages of 20 and 29 was under some form of criminal justice supervision

The criminal justice system is increasingly run as a business but, if the USA is an exemplar of what is to come, profits are guaranteed but social order is not.

Credit: The Guardian

... If the present rate of growth continues, 4.5 million black men will be in prison by the year 2020. This will be very good for the prison business. But very bad for the future of democracy.[78]

I would argue that the criminal justice system is not about paying for crime, about costs, democracy or even justice itself, because

To imagine that penal policy can be formulated or implemented according to abstract legalistic notions of justice, fairness or seriousness is ... a nonsense. It is, after all, impossible to punish crimes, we can only punish people.[79]

Figure 4.6: **Costs of penal measures**

Costs of imprisonment:

Adult male prisoner 1995/96	£ 1,776 per month
Open youth establishments	£ 2,071
Closed youth establishments	£1,730

Costs of alternatives to custody:

Probation order 1995/6	£190 per month
Community service order	£140 month
Supervision order	£ 180 per month

Source: NACRO, *Criminal Justice Digest*, February 1997.

Criminal justice is about **punishing people** – and those people are predominantly the poor, the disadvantaged and the powerless.

NOTES

1 D Cook, *Rich Law, Poor Law: different responses to tax and supplementary benefit fraud*, Open University Press, 1989, p149.

2 *Keith Committee Report on the Enforcement Powers of the Revenue Departments*, Cmnd 8822, HMSO, 1983, para 8.1.

3 *Ibid*, para 8.3.

4 J Braithwaite, *Corporate Crime in the Pharmaceutical Industry*, RKP, 1984.

5 *Ibid*.

6 D Cook, 'The role of the NRA in the regulation of water pollution: Tales of the Riverbank', unpublished paper to the British Criminology Conference, Cardiff, July 1993.

7 J Braithwaite, *Crime, Shame and Re-Integration*, Cambridge University Press, 1989; Cook, *see* note 1; H Croall, *White-Collar Crime*, Open

University Press, 1992.

8   J Braithwaite, 'Corporate crime and republican criminological praxis', in F Pearce and L Snider (eds), *Corporate Crime, Contemporary Debates*, University of Toronto Press, 1995, p54.

9   G Geis and J Dimento, 'Should we prosecute corporations and/or individuals?' in Pearce and Snider (eds), *ibid*, 1995, p84.

10   *Guardian*, 1 February 1994.

11   J Braithwaite, *Crime, Shame and Re-Integration*, see note 8.

12   W Carson, *The Other Price of Britain's Oil*, Martin Robertson, 1982; Croall, *see* note 7.

13   Croall, *see* note 7.

14   Home Office, *Digest 3: Information on the Criminal Justice System in England and Wales*, Home Office Research and Statistical Department, 1995.

15   Audit Commission, *Local Authority Performance Indicators 1994/5: crime and detection*, Vol 3, HMSO, 1996, p23.

16   D Cook, 'Fiddling tax and benefits: inculpating the poor, exculpating the rich', in P Carlen and D Cook (eds), *Paying for Crime*, Open University Press, 1989.

17   R Smith, 'Legal aid on an ebbing tide', in *Journal of Law and Society*, Vol 23, No 4, 1996.

18   D S Wall, 'Legal aid, social policy and the architecture of criminal justice', in *ibid*.

19   *Ibid*, p565.

20   Home Office, *Criminal Statistics for England and Wales: 1995*, HMSO, 1996, p221.

21   S Box, *Recession, Crime and Punishment*, Macmillan, 1987.

22   *Ibid*; C Hale, 'Economy, crime and punishment', in *Contemporary Crises*, Vol 13, No 4, 1989.

23   B Hudson, *Justice Through Punishment*, Macmillan, 1987, p95.

24   D Hood, *Race and Sentencing: a study in the Crown Court*, Clarendon Press, 1992.

25   Lord Justice Taylor, 1 July 1995.

26   NACRO, *Race Policies into Action*, Spring 1997.

27   Penal Affairs Consortium (PAC), *Race and Criminal Justice*, PAC, 1986.

28   Hood, *see* note 24; Hudson, 1987, *see* note 23.

29   PAC, *see* note 27.

30   M Fitzgerald, *Ethnic Minorities and the Criminal Justice System*, paper prepared for the Royal Commission on Criminal Procedure, HMSO, 1993.

31   C Oppenheim and L Harker, *Poverty: the facts*, CPAG Ltd, 1996.

32   B Hudson, *Penal Policy and Social Justice*, Macmillan, 1993, p73.

33   P Carlen, *Women, Crime and Poverty*, Open University Press, 1988.

34 F Heidensohn, *Women and Crime*, Macmillan, 1985, p174.
35 BBC Panorama, *Violent Women*, 11 November 1996.
36 P Carlen and A Worrall (eds), *Gender, Crime and Justice*, Open University Press, 1987.
37 H Allen, *Justice Unbalanced*, Open University Press, 1987.
38 A Worrall, *Offending Women*, Routledge, 1990, p81.
39 Home Office, *see* note 14.
40 Carlen and Worrall (eds), *see* note 36; A Worrall, *see* note 38.
41 P Carlen, 'Justice and gender: the need for reform', in L Samuelson and B Schissle (eds), *Sentencing*, Garamond Press, 1991.
42 S Brown, *Magistrates at Work*, Open University Press, 1990, pp40–41.
43 *Ibid*, p39.
44 Hood, *see* note 24.
45 *Guardian*, 27 March 1997.
46 Home Office, *see* note 14.
47 *Ibid*, p18
48 *Ibid*, p145.
49 D Moxon and C Whitaker, *Imprisonment for Fine Default*, Home Office Research and Statistics Directorate, Research Findings No 35, Home Office, 1996.
50 NAPO, *Inconsistency in Sentencing*, 1996.
51 B Hudson, 1993, *see* note 32, p87.
52 Sheldon, quoted in Hudson, *ibid*.
53 Prison Reform Trust (PRT), *The Identikit Prisoner*, PRT, 1991, p5.
54 *British Medical Journal*, 14 December 1996.
55 NACRO *Digest*, October 1996 and February 1997.
56 *Ibid*.
57 I Anderson, *Single Homeless People*, Department of the Environment, 1993.
58 *Poverty*, CPAG Ltd, Spring 1997.
59 PAC, *Housing Benefit and Prisoners*, PAC, 1995.
60 J Reiman, *The Rich Get Richer and the Poor Get Prison*, Macmillan, 1990.
61 *Ibid*, p5.
62 *Ibid*, p9.
63 Home Office, *Digest 3: Information on the Criminal Justice System in England and Wales*, Home Office Research and Statistical Department, 1995.
64 G Rusche and O Kirchheimer, *Punishment and Social Structure*, Columbia University Press, 1939.
65 *Independent*, 6 February 1997.
66 Correspondence from Prison Reform Trust, 1997.
67 *Guardian*, 28 April 1997.
68 HM Prison Service *Briefing* No 105, March 1997.

69   Ibid.
70   P Carlen, 'Why study women's imprisonment or anyone else's?', in British Journal of Criminology, Vol 34, 1994.
71   Box, see note 21, p212.
72   T Mathiesen, The Politics of Abolition: essays in political action theory, Martin Robertson, 1974.
73   Box, see note 21, p129.
74   Ibid, p26
75   Ibid; Hudson, see note 32; Downes, 'What the next government should do about crime', in The Howard Journal, Vol 36, No 1, 1997
76   Melossi, quoted in C Hale, 'Economy, crime and punishment', in Contemporary Crises, Vol 13, No 4, 1989.
77   N Christie, Crime Control and Industry, Routledge, 1993.
78   Vivien Stern, Secretary General of Penal Reform International, Guardian, 15 January 1997.
79   Hudson, see note 32, p88.

5 Crime, need and greed

> It's simply lack of money. You don't have enough to live on. You fiddle for necessities and don't look for any luxuries. (Carol, quoted in *Rich Law, Poor Law*)[1]

> Social's not giving you the money for the standard of living now, today. They're not doing it, so the choice is either to work [ie, while claiming] or crime. (Dean and Melrose, 1997)[2]

Social security fraud is overwhelmingly a crime of poverty: those who commit it are principally motivated by need rather than greed. This chapter will examine the links between crime, poverty and punishment by analysing how, as a society, we respond to those who defraud the state by fiddling social security benefits, as compared with our responses to those who defraud through tax evasion.

Although media coverage has traditionally portrayed benefit fraud as an organised crime of greed, research indicates that most 'known' social security fraud is the product of individual claimants who simply cannot make ends meet on (what are perceived as) inadequate levels of benefit. As Chapter 2 has demonstrated, the gap between rich and poor has widened dramatically since 1979. Since then the 'real' value of means-tested social security benefits has fallen and more people than ever (over 10 million people in Britain) are dependent on the 'safety net' means-tested benefit, income support. Moreover, means testing has itself intensified, accounting for 35 per cent of social security expenditure in 1995/96, compared with 16 per cent in 1979.[3]

While the poor are getting poorer, the rich are getting richer still. But, as Chapters 3 and 4 demonstrated, this does not seem to have led to a reduction in the economic crimes of the rich – and tax evasion is no exception. Despite its scale and costs, popular attitudes towards tax evasion have always been equivocal: it remains not only tolerated, but almost praised because, as Margaret Thatcher observed, it shows that 'the enterprise is still there'.[4] Even the language of tax fraud does not directly refer to its criminality: Inland Revenue investigations fall within department's 'compliance' activities and the unpaid tax collected as a result of investigation work is termed 'yield from compliance' (see Table 5.2 below). In popular and political discourse there is no direct relationship between the crime of tax fraud and its victims: it is relegated to the level of a 'victimless crime ... if they can be regarded as crimes at all', in the same league as 'taking your clothes off on remote beaches'.[5]

But there *are* victims, as the Royal Commission on the Income Tax observed in 1920:

> People must be made to understand that if they defraud the Revenue they are committing a mean and despicable offence against every one of their fellow taxpayers.

Three quarters of a century later, it appears that we have not been successful in making people understand this basic principle although we are all its victims. Paradoxically, it is the taxpayers themselves who are usually seen as victims – of the stifling, intrusive, 'intolerable inquisition' of taxation itself.[6]

GIVE AND TAKE

Whereas benefit claimants are defined as 'takers' from the state, taxpayers possess the status of 'givers'. Consequently, the taxpayer who fiddles is sympathetically seen to be refusing to pay over *their* hard-earned money to a draconian and inefficient state. Besides, the honest taxpayer who plays their full part in the 'Robin Hood' activities of a welfare state may find that their hard-earned taxes are being squandered on over-generous welfare payments to the undeserving poor: as Boyson commented, the welfare state takes from 'the energetic, successful and thrifty' to pay for the support of 'the idle, the failures and the feckless'.[7]

By contrast, when the poor (the 'idle, feckless, failures') themselves defraud the state, it is seen quite unequivocally as a 'rip-off', 'scrounging', 'fraud' or 'abuse'. The victims of this crime are similarly easy to identify:

Benefit fraud is a selfish crime which is directed against the poorest in society. It robs the system of resources which should go to those that need them. (Peter Lilley, Secretary of State for Social Security, DSS Press Release, 18 May 1994)

By sleight of hand the 'real' perpetrators and the victims of benefit fraud are readily packaged as the **undeserving** and **deserving** poor respectively.

ONE LAW FOR THE RICH?

Tax evasion is rendered a less straightfoward issue partly because of its complexity, both in law and in practice. Evasion may be a crime of omission or commission, located along a continuum of individual opportunity and culpability. Nevertheless, the *outcome* is identical to that of benefit fraud – loss to the public purse. The legal and practical complexities of the offence are well demonstrated by the Royal Commission report of 1920, as is the essence of the crime itself:

> [The taxpayer] may not always be guilty of fraud; he [sic] may be culpably careless; he may decide every doubtful point in his own favour by deliberately refraining from inquiry; he may cultivate a profitable ignorance or a negligence that is not free from guile. His conduct may, in short, occupy any position in the scale, from something less than completely honesty down to absolute fraud. The one common feature in all such cases is that the Revenue suffers, which is another way of saying that the evader contrives to make his fellow citizen pay something that ought to come out of his own pocket.[8]

In 1994/95 the amount yielded as a result of the Revenue's compliance activities peaked at over £6 billion (see Table 5.2). One could assume that, given the scale of this crime (which, in Peter Lilley's words, 'robs the system of resources') swift and punitive action would be taken against the offenders. But in that year (1994/95) the Revenue mounted only 357 criminal prosecutions, compared with 9,546 fraud prosecutions mounted by the DSS (see Table 5.1).

However, this is not the whole story: most Revenue prosecutions actually related to offences such as stealing Revenue girocheques, offences by employers and pay clerks, and frauds connected with sub-contractors tax exemption certificates. In other words, of the few Revenue prosecutions which *are* mounted, most are for offences which are closest to 'real crime', rather than for tax evasion as it is popularly understood. The number of prosecutions for submitting false claims or false accounts (in popular terms, lying in tax returns to evade taxes) amounted to just *nine* cases in 1995/96.

TABLE 5.1: **Prosecutions for tax and social security fraud.**

Year	DSS prosecutions	Inland Revenue prosecutions
1991/92	4,379	249
1992/93	5,239	217
1993/94	7,645	216
1994/95	9,546	357
1995/96	10,677	192

Sources: DSS press releases; Board of Inland Revenue annual reports.

By comparison, the majority (9,470) of the DSS prosecutions mounted in 1995/96 were of individual claimants (the remainder being cases of other and/or organised forms of fraud). Also, the amounts defrauded by those individuals who are prosecuted by the DSS are clearly limited by the levels of benefit which they can claim. But the opportunities and scale of tax frauds are not so constrained: as a result, many social security claimants are being prosecuted for defrauding amounts which district tax inspectors would consider too trivial to bother collecting.

DIFFERENTIAL 'PAY-OFF' FROM FRAUD INVESTIGATIONS

One argument for the Revenue's softly-softly approach to compliance (as opposed to adopting a 'hard' prosecution strategy), is the objective of securing repayment of taxes and ensuring that the taxpayer pays her/his taxes in full in the future. Although any full and critical discussion of the effectiveness of this strategy is beyond the scope of this chapter, suffice it to say that the Inland Revenue produces figures of the yield-cost ratios of its investigatory staff which offer one measure of their effectiveness. These figures are impressive: they demonstrate that tax inspectors based in large business offices and engaged in technical review work recouped 167 times their salary costs in 1995/96; the cost-yield ratio for special compliance officers is 16.5:1 and company accounts investigations 35:1.[9] But there is evidence that, in recent years, some of these ratios have declined as overall Revenue staffing cuts began to bite. This is supported by the fact that 1995/96 marked a significant drop (of almost a £1 billion) on the previous years total of tax yielded as a result of compliance work (see Table 5.2).

There is, however, no shortage of staffing where benefit fraud is concerned: over the last three years the number of specialist fraud staff has increased from around 3,000 to over 5,000.[10] What can be said about their cost-effectiveness? The *Benefits Agency Report* (1995) which provided Peter Lilley with his estimates of the scale of social security fraud confirmed that the cost of its fraud survey alone was £1 million, but the figures it provided do not enable us to gauge the cost-effectiveness of its investigation staff. The report also established the principles upon which its five-year anti-fraud strategy is based, the main one being the **invest to save** principle – the Department would bear the short-term costs of added investigatory efforts to produce longer-term benefit savings. This established that funding for anti-fraud work would be secured with the aim of:

> securing a reduction in benefit expenditure as a result of incorrect benefit being detected, stopped or prevented.[11]

Two thorny issues are raised here: first, how the success or failure of 'invest to save' can be properly (and independently) evaluated and secondly, the subtle inclusion of the notion of 'benefit **incorrectness**' in the Agency's anti-**fraud** strategy. The latter effectively signals a worrying blurring of the boundaries between what is fraud and what is an incorrect benefit payment. In the context of 'invest to save' this conflation may serve two functions: first, to provide dubious evidence of 'anti-fraud' savings to justify substantial investment in policing benefit fraud; secondly, in so doing to amplify the scale of the problem of 'fraud', thereby closing a circle which justified the investment in the first place!

At this point it is useful to turn to a critical examination of fraud statistics and what they can and cannot reveal about the extent of tax and social security fraud.

FRAUDULENT STATISTICS

At the 1992 Conservative Party conference, Peter Lilley won a long-standing ovation for announcing his intention to 'close down the something-for-nothing society'. In decrying welfare fraud as 'an insult to the law-abiding majority', he announced a target of £500 million of 'bogus claims' to be tracked down. Sure enough, by the following year his target had been met and exceeded (see Table 5.2). This represents a now very familiar pattern of political target-setting followed by a swift, record-breaking agency response:

> The crackdown on benefit fraud broke all records last year – with the Benefits Agency saving £654 million of taxpayers' money. (DSS Press release, 18 May 1994)

> The crackdown on benefit fraud saved the taxpayer a record £717.6 million last year. (DSS Press Release, 10 July 1995)

> Fraudulent claims for Income Support and Unemployment Benefit alone cost the taxpayer a crippling £1.4 billion a year, Peter Lilley revealed today. (DSS Press Release, 10 July 1995, reporting the findings of the Benefits Agency Review's own survey on the extent of fraud)

> An all time record of £1.4 billion pounds of taxpayers money has been saved through anti-fraud activities last year. (DSS Press Release, 5 August 1996)

It appears that the Secretary of State's targets were, by hook or by crook, going to be met by his zealous departmental officials whose own performances were, in turn, judged in terms of their personal targeted objectives (for fraud officers these are 'benefit savings'!).

'Benefit savings' are projected and not actual figures: although they claim to represent the amount of benefit saved as the result of investigation work, they are calculated on the basis of **multipliers**. For example, if an investigator discovers a case of suspected fraud and/or persuades a claimant to withdraw their claim to benefit, they will then multiply the claimant's weekly benefit by a factor of 32, on the assumption that the claim would have lasted another 32 weeks, had the investigation not taken place. As a result, a 'successful' investigation of a claimant who was, for example, receiving £100 a week in income support will lead to an official (but multiplied) benefit saving of £3,200.

A successful investigation, one which leads to benefit savings (and is subject to a 32 week multiplier), may not involve any fraud at all: rule changes since 1989 have expanded what 'counts' as fraud to include payment **irregularities**: this category may lead to a

blurring of the boundaries between the illegal and the merely
incompetent or ill-advised. Nevertheless, these changes undoubtedly
swell estimates of benefit savings which are allegedly achieved as a
result of 'fraud' investigations.

TABLE 5.2: **DSS and tax fraud**

Year	Benefit 'savings' (multiplied) in £ millions	Yield (actual) from compliance in £ millions
1991/92	446	4,905
1992/93	558	4,575
1993/94	654	4,697
1994/95	717	6,118
1995/96	1,222*	5,242

* This is a revision of the DSS press release figure of £1.4 billion, which included local
authority housing benefit fraud, not included in earlier years.

Sources: DSS press releases; Board of Inland Revenue annual reports.

The empirical basis for the use of multipliers is unclear and the figure
itself may vary – from the 22-week claim assumed by the Employment
Service, to the 32-week multiplier used for income support. But,
regardless of their technical origins, they raise two crucial issues
concerning both law and ideology. First, fraud estimates using
calculations of 'benefit savings' involve costing of fraud on the basis of
a **projection** of the crime (for eight months) into the future. In all
other fields of criminal activity the traditional measure of the costs of
a crime is clearly **retrospective** and, at the individual level, usually
means 'taking into consideration' (TIC) past, admitted offences. Social
security fraud is the only crime I am aware of where issues such as
evidence, proof, guilt and personal admission are all absent from the
formal calculations of the extent of the individual's lawbreaking.

Second, the use of multipliers has had a **ratchet effect** on
estimates of the scale of fraud: as the press releases quoted earlier
indicate, the political stakes are raised ever-higher along with the
benefit savings targets announced annually and lauded at party
conferences. In the context of public spending cuts and a very large
social security budget (amounting to £91 billion last year), the
political imperative to cut costs through anti-fraud drives is stronger.
At the same time, exaggerated estimates of the scale of benefit

'scrounging' have wider social effects, including:

- an adverse effect on benefit take-up rates;
- undermining public support for the 'welfare state' in general;
- undermining support for welfare provision, in particular for those groups targeted as fraud-prone (including lone mothers and asylum-seekers – see Chapter 7 below).

Amplification of the scale of fraud has also been accomplished by the inclusion of 'other' forms of benefit fraud within the overall DSS figures: for example, housing benefit fraud was included for the first time in 1995/96 (as Table 5.2 indicates). The press widely failed to distinguish this when quoting the 'official' figure of £1.4 billion fraud savings, and so reflected a distorted picture of the upward trend of social security fraud.

THE POLITICS OF 'SCROUNGING'

It could be argued that given the political imperative to cut spiralling welfare expenditure, an emphasis on the ever-increasing costs of 'scrounging' serves a useful deterrent function. An anti-scrounger strategy, on the surface geared to deterring fraudulent claims, may also deter legitimate claimants and so cut welfare costs. It also builds on historic divisions between the deserving and undeserving poor: 'every pound lost to fraud means less for those in *real* need' (Peter Lilley, 7 October, 1992, emphasis added).

At a more base level, this political emphasis generates a powerful popular response, as the *Daily Star* headline 'Stuff the Spongers' demonstrates.[12] Ultimately, the anti-scrounger strategy justifies cuts in benefits for, and the increased policing of, those groups who are seen as the new undeserving poor.

If there is a genuine political drive to deter fraud and to save the honest taxpayer's money, then why not pursue the far richer pickings available from tax fraud? Even if we were to accept the official (grossly exaggerated) estimates of benefit fraud, they still remain dwarfed by the scale of tax fraud: the actual yield achieved as a result of the Inland Revenue's compliance activities was £6.1 billion in 1994/95 (or, around 3p off the basic rate of income tax). To address this question, and to understand the context in which social security fraud and tax evasion are treated so differently, we need to turn our attention to broader political priorities and the need to 'get elected'.

TAXATION, WELFARE AND GETTING ELECTED

The political prioritisation of social security fraud is by no means new.[13] Although 'scroungermania' reached a new height in the 1970s, the Thatcher era signalled important changes in both the intensity and direction of anti-fraud policy. For example, the use of special squads (Special Claims Control Units – SCCU), random checks on target groups (particularly the unemployed and lone mothers) and the introduction of the principle of targeting 'benefit savings' all raised the stakes in policing of welfare claimants.[14] These changes were produced in the context of New Right political principles which inextricably linked welfare with the issue of personal taxation. Put simply, it was argued that the state (and the hard-pressed taxpayer) could not 'afford' the welfare state. At the same time, personal taxes were seen to stifle enterprise and effort, and so should be reduced to offer greater incentives.

The political goal of reducing personal taxation has remained virtually unchallenged since the election of Margaret Thatcher in 1979. With the notable (and recent) exception of the Liberal Democrats, politicians have increasingly vied to distance themselves from any notion of progressive or redistributive taxation and, instead, have engaged in a political 'Dutch auction' in an attempt to demonstrate their commitment to 'low taxes'. Undoubtedly the charge that Labour was the 'party of high taxation' played a significant part in their 1992 election defeat. Consequently, low taxation has become central to the political canon of both major parties (one which was reflected in both the Labour and Conservative parties' 1997 election manifestos).

However, in the case of the Conservatives, the political prioritising of low taxes assumes an almost moral quality: previously allied to broader (Thatcherite) goals of 'rolling back the frontiers of the state', maintaining incentives to effort, and promoting the 'enterprise culture', this commitment to low taxation proved to be a central plank in successive (and successful) Conservative election campaigns.

But, as argued in Chapter 2, the success of any incentive to enterprise ultimately depends on a parallel disincentive to dependency. In these terms, 'getting elected' involves putting in place social and fiscal policies to **stimulate the winners** and **stigmatise the losers** and this has been principally achieved through **taxation and welfare policies**: they have provided the means through which enterprise has been lauded and promoted, and economic dependency castigated and deterred. One means of achieving the former may have been by, politically, turning a blind eye to tax evasion in the interests of individual 'enterprise'. The latter has been promoted through the stereotype of the social security 'scrounger'.

At the time of writing the first draft of this chapter, the 1996 Budget was announced. Its implications for the treatment of tax and social security fraud appeared significant, particularly in the emphasis which was placed on tackling tax evasion. At first sight Chancellor Kenneth Clarke's promises were impressive: the 'invest to save' principle was to be extended as part of the 'continuing fight against tax and benefit fraud and tax loopholes'. But when both the departmental texts and the practical measures to be put in place were analysed in more depth, there seemed little scope for optimism. For example, to quote from official press releases:

> As part of the Government's initiative to crackdown more widely on fraud and evasion, the Inland Revenue will be deploying up to 2,000 more staff over the next three years to counter tax evasion and avoidance.

On reading the fine print we find that this means 1,000 tax inspectors and other staff will be 'deployed' on compliance work and 1,000 'who would otherwise not be needed will be re-deployed'. (This needs to be set in the context of a 12,500 reduction in Revenue staffing over the past four years.)

On the commitment to invest to save the taxpayers' money through tackling tax, VAT and social security fraud, it was announced that:

> The 'Spend to Save' package will cost £800 million over the next 3 years to secure, in a well-planned way, revenue and expenditure savings of well over eight times that amount at £6.7 billion.

But, on closer inspection, the amount 'spent to save' by the three main departments in tackling tax, VAT and benefit fraud over the next three years will be:

Inland Revenue	£190 million
Customs and Excise	£88 million
DSS	£470 million

Clearly, the political emphasis on social security remains pre-eminent in real terms – in terms of government resources – and there is little evidence that this is likely to change under New Labour. According to recent press releases, new Social Security Minister Frank Field promises to be 'tougher' than his predecessors:

> We are most grateful for what the last government did, but it's the beginning of the story, not the end. (Frank Field, quoted in *The Times*, 9 May 1997)

This is not to say that any shift towards admitting the seriousness of tax fraud is not extremely welcome – it certainly is! But its symbolic importance could prove greater than its fiscal impact – in the last Budget before a general election (and with increasing public concern over 'fat cats' and 'sleaze'), it could be argued that Clarke's apparent onslaught on tax fraud was an electioneering strategy (albeit an unsuccessful one). As for the likely direction and outcomes of an anti-fraud stragegy under New Labour, we will have to wait and see.

HOTLINES AND BILLBOARD POLITICS

So, what's new? Tax evasion remains a largely invisible crime (despite the pronouncements in the 1996 Budget) and the political profile of social security fraud seems as high as ever (despite a change of government). The disparity in responses to what are essentially crimes of need and crimes of greed is all too evident, as the following example shows.

Last summer (1996) I drove past two government-sponsored billboards: they were located close to one another, along the same busy northern city street, but conveyed very different messages about what it means to be a social security claimant and a taxpayer in contemporary Britain.

Billboard number one read: 'IF YOU KNOW OF A BENEFIT RIP-OFF, GIVE US A TELEPHONE TIP-OFF.' A free hotline number was then given, for onlookers to call in with information.

Billboard number two took the form of a humorous cartoon of the 'taxman': this character is used widely in television and other media campaigns (especially those centring on the move to self-assessment in 1997). In the wake of the Euro 1996 football competition, this poster showed the middle-aged, plump, bowler-hatted and moustached taxman poised (partially clad) as goalkeeper in a football goal. The one-liner accompanying this cartoon invited the onlooker to 'AVOID PENALTIES', and supplied a free hotline number for taxpayers to seek advice and information on self-assessment and avoiding the Inland Revenue's financial penalties.

The 'shop a cheat' hotline advertised on the first billboard was, ironically, launched in the same month as the closure of a DSS advice line, and as out-of-hours emergency services for claimants were being withdrawn: these cuts, together with curtailing mobile 'benefit buses' for advice and ending benefit offices' extended opening hours, were officially referred to as affecting the 'luxury end of customer service'.[15] However, with an estimated £1.5 to £3 billion in benefits remaining unclaimed each year, advice on entitlement should hardly be referred to as a 'luxury' which we cannot afford.

An alternative and critical view was expressed by a leading civil service trades union representative, who argued that such cuts are part of 'a scorched earth policy' against the poor and the vulnerable.[16] He also noted that the running costs of the 'beat-a-cheat' hotline are all the more questionable when seen in the context of an overall cut of 25 per cent in the social security administrative budget over the next two years, which will clearly impact on services to *all* claimants.[17]

By contrast, the second billboard demonstrates that the Inland Revenue is committed to supporting and advising taxpayers, particularly in the light of the move to self-assessment. More importantly, the juxtaposition of these two advertisements sheds much light on deeper attitudes to tax and welfare: the 'taxman' is a figure of fun, because we all know (with a nudge and a wink) that nobody likes paying taxes. The benefit claimant is, by definition, a target for suspicion and surveillance because we all know (with a sneer) that most are 'on the scrounge'. These ideas and images have serious political effects: they enable and justify unequal responses to those who fiddle taxes and welfare benefits, and so sustain deep social divisions.

FRAUD CAMPAIGNS

The DSS fraud hotline was piloted as part of a series of 'spotlight campaigns' involving investigatory blitzes on 21 targeted districts. These campaigns are reminiscent of the Special Claims Control Unit (SCCU) 'swoops' of the early 1980s, which were officially stopped in 1986 following allegations that officers harassed (female) claimants, that unacceptable investigatory techniques were used and

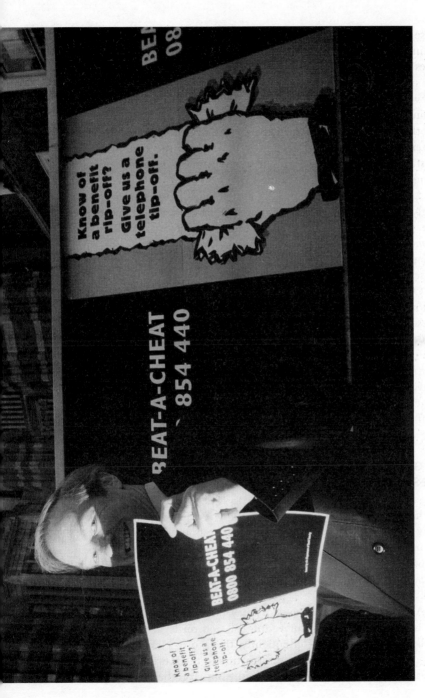

Social Security Secretary Peter Lilley launched the benefit fraud hotline in August 1996, having just closed the DSS phone line which gave free advice to claimants.

Credit: The Guardian

false allegations made to encourage claimants to withdraw their claims to benefit.[18] A decade after SCCU was wound up, its legacy lives on in the spotlight campaigns' 'blitz' and random investigation of suspect claimant groups. Although no detailed figures were provided on the outcome of the 21 pilots, official press releases claimed that they 'more than paid for' the cost of the exercise. The spotlight campaigns, in turn, paved the way for the high-profile extension of similar hotlines across the UK, and the 'benefit rip-off' poster campaign of the summer was replicated in local newspaper campaigns throughout the winter of 1996/97.

At the same time, recent DSS anti-fraud initiatives have increasingly adopted a multi-agency approach, involving local authorities, the Contribution Agency and Child Support Agency. The trend towards 'data matching' has increased the possibilities for interagency fraud work, although it has also raised civil liberties issues (discussed further in Chapter 7).

On 1 April 1996, those Benefits Agency staff involved in investigatory work merged with Employment Services counterparts, and these 5,000 (plus) investigators are now separately managed by fraud managers, outside of the Benefit Agency local office framework. This is the logical outcome of policies which have, over the past five years, increasingly 'ring-fenced' fraud work (although this shift has had worrying implications for other Benefits Agency staff in local offices who find themselves increasingly overstretched as a result of staff cuts, which will intensify over the next two years).

RIGHTS, DUTIES AND INDIVIDUAL RESPONSIBILITY

Although history teaches us that nothing is really 'new', one *relatively* new theme in the analysis of unequal responses to tax and social security fraud centres on differing perceptions of the duties and responsibilities of the taxpayer and the claimant in providing full and accurate information to government departments – the Revenue and DSS respectively.

As argued earlier, tax evasion may take the form of a crime of omission (of full and accurate information on legal tax liability) as well as commission. Consequently, the more a taxpayer has the opportunity to 'omit' giving information to the Revenue, the greater are the possibilities for evasion as 'omission'. It is therefore important to note the implications of recent Revenue moves towards **self-assessment** for individual taxpayers. Of course, trading taxpayers and businesses already, in practice, 'self-assess' by providing annual accounts of income and expenditure, but in 1997 self-assessment will be extended to all those who are required to fill in annual tax returns. History tells us the effect this is likely to have on opportunities for evasion:

> In the sphere in which self-assessment is requisite, there is a substantial amount of fraud and evasion.[19]

Self-assessment will also open up possibilities for (legal) tax avoidance, through the use of tax planning advisers and accountants who will increasingly be called to help individuals self-assess their tax liability: it has long been recognised that 'evasion is illegal, although in practice this usually means that the avoider could afford an accountant and the evader could not'.[20] What is new is that self-assessment makes both crimes of omission and tax avoidance through 'tax planning' even more likely.

For social security claimants, the duty to provide full information has very different effects. Traditionally, claimants provided verification of details of their claim wherever possible (for instance, wage slips, child benefit order books, rent books and bank books, where appropriate) although, in practice, social security officials frequently sought verification on the claimant's behalf. However, under the guise of administrative efficiency, new rules are being introduced to place the onus of proof squarely on the claimant.

> The customer must actively help. Where information that was reasonably required was not forthcoming, it would be appropriate to apply a sanction such as limiting the start date of entitlement to the date on which it was supplied.[21]

As a spokeswoman for the National Association for Citizens' Advice Bureaux commented in response,

> People will not get the money to which they are entitled because they may not be able to produce information from a former employer or a mortgage company, or they may have problems making a claim because they are homeless or mentally ill.[22]

To summarise, the ways in which the duties of taxpayer and claimant are realised through official departmental policies mean that the taxpayer is likely to be given the **benefit of the doubt**, whereas the social security claimant is not. This marked shift of the burden of proof to the social security 'customer' marks the extension of a principle which has been successfully applied to asylum-seekers in recent years – the presumption of non-entitlement until **genuine** entitlement (in the case of asylum-seekers the word 'innocence' may be more apt) has been proven (see Chapter 7 for a fuller discussion of recent immigration legislation and the criminalisation of members of visible minority ethnic groups).

TARGETING 'FRAUD-PRONE' GROUPS

As I will argue in Chapter 7, immigration, welfare, child support and anti-fraud policies have all combined to produce an ideological and political climate which enables the intensive policing of marginalised groups – particularly minority ethnic groups and lone mothers.

Where minority ethnic groups are concerned, the term '**welfare policing**' could be used to describe the role that a variety of state agencies have been forced to assume under the Asylum and Immigration Act 1996. Under its provisions, headteachers, hospital administrators, housing and social security staff are encouraged (and trained) to identify suspected illegal immigrants and report them to the Home Office. The Social Security Advisory Committee (SSAC) pointed out likely consequences for any non-white benefit claimant, as the changes

> were likely to impact on a far wider group than intended … they would lead to benefit claims from black and other ethnic minority claimants being subjected to particular scrutiny.[23]

In responding to the concerns of the SSAC, the Secretary of State justified the draconian provisions of the Act in terms of public reluctance to support asylum-seekers.

> It is clear from the significant level of correspondence received, especially when well-documented *abuses* of the system come into the public domain, that the current degree and extent of assistance given to asylum seekers lacks public support.[24] (emphasis added)

But there is evidence that details of those 'well-documented abuses of the system' were deliberately leaked by the Home Office.[25] Moreover, it is significant that the stereotype of the 'bogus' asylum-seeker had figured prominently in successive Tory Party conference speeches which all called for a 'crackdown' on scroungers. In this way the insidious connections between 'race', immigration and benefit fraud were established in the public mind.

Where lone mothers are concerned, the handling of what used to be termed 'liable relative' cases has always been intrusive: social security officers were obliged to question mothers on intimate details of their relationships with 'putative fathers' and SCCU officers took this a stage further by targeting lone mothers as, by definition, fraud-prone. In the early 1980s, SCCU activities involved unannounced home visits and surveillance, and 'excessive' techniques of interrogation.[26] Once again, recent child support and anti-fraud policies have accentuated the degree of welfare policing of lone mothers.

Although the male-breadwinner/female-dependant relationship which the welfare state has assumed since Beveridge fails to come to terms with changing family formations (and mass unemployment), it continues to underpin social security policy, in the form of the Child Support Act. Its provisions assume that lone mothers will be willing and able to name the fathers of their children, to enable 'errant fathers' to be pursued for state maintenance, with the penalty of a 20 per cent deduction from the benefits of unco-operative lone mothers. This deduction, 20 per cent for six months and 10 per cent for a year thereafter, is a punitive and disciplinary mechanism which fails to take account of many women's legitimate concerns about retaining contact with former partners (who may, for instance, have been threatening or violent).

Lone mothers on welfare have long been regarded as fraud-prone.[27] But the 1990s have seen a hardening of political attitudes and an intensification of their 'target' status. This has been justified on the basis of highly questionable evidence. Based on very dubious methodology, the Benefits Agency's Benefits Review crassly stated that 'the level of fraud in lone parent cases was 18.6 per cent', an assertion which was widely reported in the media.[28] In fact, this figure was based on assumptions about just 101 lone parent cases (out of a total of 690 reviewed) which according to investigators exhibited 'strong suspicion', but *no proof*, of fraud.[29] Nonetheless, this 'evidence' has been used, together with recent CSA research, to justify a proposal to double the financial penalty to 40 per cent, indefinitely, for lone mothers who fail to comply with their Benefits Agency and Child Support Agency regulators.

The inappropriateness of financial penalties for 'non-compliant' lone mothers is deeply ironic: those women who *do* commit benefit fraud are often driven to do so by the inadequacy of benefit levels and depth of their poverty. As David Donnison tellingly observes:

> Women are irrevocably condemned to debt. Some of them cope ... but many have to make a stark choice: between risking their health and the health of their children in cold, damp flats; or paying an electrician to by-pass the meter; or getting a job and concealing their earnings from tax and social security officials; or forming a relationship with a man whose contributions to the household are likewise concealed; or stealing food and clothing from shops; or borrowing money at crucifying interest rates from illicit lenders who employ their local hard men to collect debts ... Which option would you choose?[30]

SUMMARY

To return to the opening of this chapter, social security fraud is primarily a crime of poverty. As already argued in Chapter 3, to say that poverty is a **source** of crime does not **excuse** it – but it does help to **explain** it. This explanation must form the basis of any sensible anti-fraud policy, which would have to be based on preventing the offending in the first place – offending which is most often explained in terms of need and the inadequacy of current benefit levels to meet the needs of many families in contemporary Britain. But this analysis needs to be supplemented by two other arguments made in this chapter:

- when we compare the policing and investigation of tax evasion with that of social security fraud (see also Chapter 4), we have evidence of '**one law for the rich, another for the poor**';
- the ways in which benefit claimants – particularly lone mothers and minority ethnic groups – are stereotyped as 'scroungers' serves to both **marginalise and criminalise** these groups, rendering them doubly excluded from full social citizenship (a theme to be discussed further in Chapter 7).

NOTES

1   D Cook, *Rich Law, Poor Law: different responses to tax and supplementary benefit fraud*, Open University Press, 1989, p87.

2   H Dean and M Melrose, 'Manageable discord: fraud and resistance in the social security system', in *Social Policy and Administration*, Vol 31, No 2, 1996.

3   *Benefits*, 1996, p39.

4   Cook, *see* note 1, p63.

5   B Bracewell-Milnes, 'Is tax avoidance/evation a burden on the taxpayer?' in A Seldon (ed), *Tax Avoision*, IEA, 1979, p112.

6   *Report of the Royal Commission on the Income Tax*, 1920, p139.

7   R Boyson, *Down With the Poor*, Churchill Press, 1971.

8   *Report of the Royal Commission on the Income Tax*, 1920, (Cmnd 615), p135.

9   Board of Inland Revenue, *Report for Year Ending 31.3.96*, Cmnd 3446, HMSO, 1996.

10 DSS Press Releases, 1993, 1996

11 Benefits Agency, *Benefits Agency Security Strategy: 5 Year Plan against fraud and abuse*, 1995, p5.

12 *Daily Star*, 8 October 1992.

13 P Golding and S Middleton, *Images of Welfare*, Martin Robertson, 1982

14 D Cook, 'Fiddling tax and benefits: inculpating the poor, exculpating the rich', in P Carlen and D Cook (eds), *Paying for Crime*, Open University Press, 1989.

15 *Guardian*, 1 March 1996.

16 *Poverty*, CPAG Ltd, Spring 1997.

17 *Ibid*.

18 Cook, *see* note 1, p141.

19 Departmental Commission of 1905, quoted in *Report of the Royal Commission on the Income Tax*, 1920, p629.

20 *Observer*, 1 February 1976, quoted in Deacon and Sinfield, 1977.

21 DSS consultation paper, Cm3328.

22 *Guardian*, 24 July 1996.

23 *Benefits*, Issue 16, 1996, p31.

24 *Ibid*.

25 *Guardian*, 16 December 1995.

26 Cook, *see* note 1.

27 D Cook, 'Women on welfare: in crime or injustice?' in P Carlen and A Worrall (eds), *Gender, Crime and Justice*, Open University Press, 1987.

28 Benefits Agency, *see* note 11, p3.

29 *Ibid*, p21.

30 D Donnison, 'Crime and Social Policy', paper to the International Conference on Crime and Social Policy, NACRO, 1992.

6 Poverty and victimisation

INTRODUCTION

> We are not all equally threatened by crime ... The poor suffer
> disproportionately from all the more serious forms of crime, the
> middle income brackets suffer more than the rich, the rich suffer
> only in terms of the least serious forms of crime and those whose
> impact they can endure, because they are well-heeled and well-
> insured. (Young and Lea)[1]

This chapter will look at the relationship between crime and poverty
by examining patterns of criminal victimisation and anxieties about
crime. As Young and Lea state, the poor suffer more from crime and
are least able to withstand its financial consequences. Drawing on
evidence from the British crime surveys, discussed in Chapter 3,
and a recent local study of crime and victimisation (Wolverhampton
Crime Audit, 1996), the chapter will focus on four themes:

- **What is known about patterns of victimisation?** Social and
  spatial issues;
- **Crime, anxiety and locality** – social and spatial factors in
  patterns of crime and victimisation;
- **Hidden victims** – following on from Chapter 3, a brief discussion
  of what is *not* known about victimisation;
- **The myth of the equal victim** – Poverty, power and 'insurance'.

PATTERNS OF VICTIMISATION: THE BRITISH CRIME SURVEY, 1996

The 1996 British Crime Survey (BCS)[2] provides data on both victimisation (during the previous year, 1995) and fear of crime for the 16,500 adults in England and Wales who formed the basis of the survey sample. The BCS, in common with all victim surveys, has inherent weaknesses. The robustness of its findings partly depends on methodological factors, notably that:

- the individuals surveyed can accurately recall events which have taken place during the past year;
- they fully understand both the language and the categorisations employed in the survey;
- they grasp and share the same meanings as those asking the questions (about particular actions and events);
- they are accurate and honest in their responses;
- they constitute a representative sample of the whole population;
- the rate of response to the survey is sufficient from which to make generalisable observations.

But victim surveys are open to the more general criticism that they inevitably stress **crime with victims** (victims who are, in addition, aware of their victimisation). This has the effect of precluding most white-collar, corporate and so-called 'victimless' crimes. In so doing, such surveys can reinforce pre-existing definitions of what 'the crime problem' is, and fail to address any alternative crime agenda (for example, see the note about 'mugging' below).

Given these reservations, the BCS does offer an important and systematic source of crime data to supplement official Home Office crime statistics. What do these surveys tell us about patterns of victimisation? First, they enable us to make some assessment of **who is most at risk** of certain offences, and who is least at risk.

In relation to violent crime, 5.2 per cent of adults surveyed were victims of one or more types of contact crime in 1995. For the BCS, the category of contact crime includes:

- **domestic violence** – incidents involving partners, ex-partners and household members and relatives;
- **mugging**★ (see p120) – all robberies, attempted robberies and snatch thefts, irrespective of any acquaintance between victim and offender;

- **stranger violence** – all violence other than mugging, in which the victim knew none of the offenders;
- **acquaintance violence** – all violence other than mugging, in which the victim knew one or more of the offenders by sight (but excluding domestic violence).

The **risks of contact crime were highest** for the following groups:

- men (6.7 per cent);
- those under 30 years of age (13.2 per cent);
- those living in London and the West Midlands;
- those living in inner city areas;
- those living in privately rented accommodation.

Those with the **lowest risk of contact crime** lived in the East Midlands and East Anglia, in non-inner city areas and in owner-occupied accommodation. In other words, the risk of contact crime is patterned according to age, sex, area and housing type – all of these factors combine to disfavour the poorer urban dwelling young male.

In relation to **burglary**, 6.3 per cent of households experienced a burglary (or an attempt) during 1995. Some victims – 12 per cent – suffered two burglaries, and 7 per cent suffered three or more incidents. The total number of incidents of burglary per 100 of the population was 8.3 in 1995. But the risks were very unevenly distributed among the population. The **risks were highest** for households:

- in the north and Greater London areas;
- in inner city areas;
- living in rented accommodation;
- living in flats rather than houses;
- with lower levels of disposable income;
- with single-adult heads of household;
- with younger heads of household;
- without household insurance.

Here the relationship between poverty and victimisation is even clearer, with the young, urban poor suffering disproportionately

---

★ The category of 'mugging' presents definitional and theoretical problems which cannot be fully explored here: the term can be seen to convey very particular meanings about the nature of the threat posed by this offence and about the stereotype of the offender involved. As such its use in crime surveys remains contested (see Hall, 1978; Stubbs, 1987).[3]

from burglary, and least able to insure against their losses. The additional factors of single parenthood, low income and flat residence signify the possibility of particular risks for lone mothers on welfare.

According to the BCS there were 4.2 million theft-related offences involving cars in 1995. In total, 23 per cent of all offences recorded by the BCS were thefts involving vehicles: **theft from vehicles** accounted for 13 per cent of all offences; **theft of vehicles** 3 per cent and attempted thefts 7 per cent. Risks of car crime were **highest** for:

- the northern regions of the country;
- inner city areas;
- those in flats and terraced houses;
- young households;
- better-off households.

Risks were **lower** for:

- the East Midlands and East Anglia;
- detached and semi-detached houses (probably more likely to have garages or private parking);
- poorer households (perhaps because their cars are less attractive to thieves).

Here the links between poverty, wealth and victimisation are more complex. On the one hand, poorer **groups** suffer less because they are less likely to be car owners and, if they are, their cars are likely to be inexpensive. But on the other, some poorer **areas** suffer more. (The relationships between issues of crime, anxiety, deprivation and locality will be explored later.)

PATTERNS OF VICTIMISATION: THE WOLVERHAMPTON CRIME AUDIT[4]

Wolverhampton is a West Midlands town which includes areas with many of the 'at risk' characteristics identified by the BCS. The findings of the recent crime audit may shed light on the relationships between locality, poverty and victimisation in the town. It should be stressed that the Audit was precisely that – a stocktaking of all available data on crime and victimisation: *recorded* crime and victim data was supplied by the West Midlands police. The Audit also drew on the findings of a recent poverty study which had questioned a sample of Wolverhampton residents on a range of issues including lifestyle, crime, victimisation and the fear of crime.

One of the aims of the Wolverhampton Crime Audit was to investigate if and how social deprivation was linked to patterns of **recorded crime and victimisation**.

In order to accomplish this, household data from the 1991 Census, together with and a variety of social deprivation indices which were 'mapped' onto the Wolverhampton police beat boundaries within which crime was recorded. Social deprivation indices used included the Townsend, Carstairs, Jarman and Department of the Environment — DoEZ (for details of what each index measures, see Appendix 1). This mapping process enabled an analysis of **social, spatial and recorded crime patterns**. The results of these analyses are broadly in line with the BCS findings, but before discussing them, it is first necessary to locate the town, and hence the crime audit, in its social and economic context.

Wolverhampton has a population estimated in 1994 to total 245,000. Recent research[5] documented the nature and the extent of poverty in the borough. Some of its key findings, against which we should set the Audit findings, are:

- Wolverhampton's unemployment rate in April 1996 was officially 12.2 per cent (compared with 10.8 per cent for the West Midlands County area and 9.1 per cent for Britain overall);
- 40 per cent of the unemployed in Wolverhampton had been without work for over a year, and 23 per cent for two years or more;
- in April 1996, 30 per cent of the 16-24 years age group was unemployed;
- according to the 1991 Census, minority ethnic groups accounted for 18.5 per cent of the population of Wolverhampton (compared with 5.5 per cent of the UK population as a whole), of whom nearly 13 per cent classified themselves as 'Asian' and 5 per cent 'Black' (the latter respondents categorising themselves as Black, Black Caribbean or Black — other);
- according to the 1991 Census, the unemployment rate for the minority ethnic population of Wolverhampton was 22 per cent (compared with the then local average of 14 per cent);
- 34 per cent of all households rent their homes from the council;
- 70 per cent of council tenants (22,150) receive housing benefit;
- a quarter of workers in Wolverhampton earn £4 an hour or less;

- 21 per cent of the adult population of Wolverhampton receives income support;
- almost one in four children in Wolverhampton receives free school meals;
- it is estimated that nearly £19 million a year in benefits is unclaimed in Wolverhampton.

Against this background, we were able to analyse selected victim data for Wolverhampton by age, gender, ethnicity★ and against indices of social deprivation. Victim data for the following crimes formed the basis of our analysis:

- burglary in dwellings;
- theft from the person and street robbery;
- wounding offences.

Not surprisingly, in relation to **household burglary** there is a predominance of male over female victims (especially within the Asian population) which may well be a reflection of householder status.

Victims of **theft from the person and street robbery** were more likely to be: white males, younger men (aged 15–24 years) and older women (aged over 50 years). Where Asian groups are concerned, there is more evenness between victimisation between the sexes. In other words, Asian women are nearly as likely as their male counterparts to be victims of theft from the person and street robbery, whereas white women are markedly less likely than their white male counterparts to be victims of this type of crime.

The peak age for victims of wounding was 18 to 24 years, and victims are typically male. Analysis of wounding victims by ethnicity and gender reveals that, where males are concerned:

- 'Black' males are least likely to be victims of wounding (their victimisation being roughly in accordance with their proportion in the overall population);
- there are 21 per cent more white male victims of wounding than would be expected; *but*
- there are 52 per cent more Asian male victims of wounding than would be expected from their frequency in the overall population.

As far as female victims of wounding are concerned, the situation is the complete reverse of their male counterparts with Asian females

---

★ See Appendix 2 for details of ethnicity classifications used in the Audit.

least, and Black women most, likely to be victims of wounding (although such offences occurred infrequently). Nonetheless, any assessment of female victimisation based on recorded crime must be treated extremely cautiously, because of the extent of hidden crimes of violence against women (see below).

The Wolverhampton Crime Audit findings to a large extent echo those of the BCS in relation to the impact of location and deprivation on patterns of crime and victimisation. We found that those police beats with highest deprivation 'scores' were those with highest rates of recorded crime.[6] This is not to say that deprivation *causes* crime but, rather, that crime and the fear of crime is an important part of the lived experience of many individuals and families in Wolverhampton – and that this experience is **patterned both spatially and socially**.

CRIME, ANXIETY AND LOCALITY

The Wolverhampton Audit found that the recorded offence rates for many different types of crime were positively linked (statistically correlated) with social deprivation indicators. But it is important to stress that levels of crime and victimisation can *themselves* form part of any sense of social and economic well-being in a particular area. In other words, crime and victimisation form an important factor shaping the way people feel about localities. These perceptions go on to have material effects – for example, in terms of policing strategy, insurance rates, housing tenure patterns, 'turnover' of residents and so on (see Chapter 1). A locality's 'reputation' for crime, whether 'justified' or not, therefore becomes a social indicator in itself. This vicious (and self-fulfilling) circle is a difficult one to break. Recent attempts to develop an ideal index of socio-economic conditions include crime rates as a crucial variable.[7]

In the Wolverhampton study the degree of correlation between certain types of crime and social deprivation was striking: in the case of **violence against the person**, the recorded crime rates for 1994/95 showed a correlation of 0.8 or more with all four indices of deprivation that were used (+1 would indicate a perfect, positive correlation). In the case of household burglaries in 1995/96, the correlations between crime rates and deprivation range between 0.61 and 0.68 (using the Townsend and Carstairs index respectively). In cases of criminal damage the correlations are even stronger –

from 0.68 to 0.71 (using Carstairs and DoEZ indicators). In short, this evidence suggests that the most socially deprived beats in the town suffer disproportionate recorded rates of violence, criminal damage and domestic burglary.[8]

But the association between rates of crime, victimisation and deprivation does not stop there. The Wolverhampton study was using figures of **recorded** crime: as Chapter 3 argued, the poor may be least likely to report crime (particularly victimless crimes like criminal damage and household burglaries where they are least likely to be insured). This means that **actual** rates of crime and victimisation would probably be even more strongly correlated with poverty and deprivation.

To what extent is anxiety about crime related to locality and to the risk of victimisation? The BCS and Wolverhampton studies arrive at similar conclusions – that worry about crime is very often firmly grounded in an individual's own experience and knowledge. Therefore, contrary to the earliest BCS findings, most anxiety about crime is not 'irrational'. Not surprisingly then, income and 'class' differences (in addition to age, gender and ethnicity) can accentuate anxieties about crime.

Recent Home Office research[9] provided a detailed 'stocktaking' and reassessment of knowledge about fear of crime gained through the British Crime Surveys 1982–1994. The summary findings were that:

- in general, people worry most about burglary, rape and vehicle crime;
- the elderly feel much less safe than other groups when out alone at night, and are a little more worried about mugging, but less worried about vehicle crime and rape, than other age groups;
- women are more worried about mugging than men and feel more unsafe when out alone at night (but men worry more than women about car crime);
- since 1984, worry about vehicle crime has risen sharply, worry about burglary has risen (but less so);
- *in general*, people felt no more unsafe in 1994 when out alone at night than they did in 1982;
- direct experience of, and knowing victims of, crime fuel people's own worry about crime;
- those who are physically vulnerable (because of their size or lack of confidence) worry more about violent crime;

- between 1 and 2 per cent of the population never go out after dark, due to fear of crime.

The 1996 BCS findings were in the main similar, but additional issues raised were that:

- 47 per cent of women and 15 per cent of men surveyed said they would feel very or a bit unsafe walking alone in their area after dark;
- 3 per cent of women never go out after dark for fear of crime, but this applied to 17 per cent of women over 60 in inner cities;
- although there was a small drop in anxiety about crime from 1994, only 4 per cent of respondents said crime had fallen in the past two years in the country as a whole. It might be that the 'crime climate' locally is more important in influencing attitudes towards crime.[10]

The BCS findings are echoed in the recent Wolverhampton Poverty Research Study.[11] The study found that when asked to identify problems which they or members of their household faced, the most commonly identified problem (40 per cent) was fear of crime and violence. This was ranked above 'making ends meet' (34 per cent) and unemployment (30 per cent). In addition to fear of crime, the linked problem of racial harassment was cited by 24 per cent of 'Black' and 23 per cent of Asian respondents to the Wolverhampton Study (see Chapter 3 for discussion of racially motivated incidents). Its evidence also supported BCS findings that a lack of insurance cover increased the potential for non-reporting of domestic burglaries.

In summary, the **risks** of an individual becoming the victim of crime vary considerably depending upon where they live (particularly if in an inner city area), their age, gender and lifestyle. At the same time, their **anxiety** about crime is also shaped by issues of age, gender, 'race' and locality. But these two dimensions cannot be entirely separated: they fuse at the point of the **locality** in which crime and deprivation is experienced, and this can, in turn, lead to a 'spiral of decline'.

> It seems probable that fear is itself often criminogenic. It can lead to spirals of decline involving the abandonment of urban public space, disinvestment and the progressive segregation of the affluent and the poor in large cities.[12]

HIDDEN VICTIMS

As already argued in Chapter 3, there is substantial under-reporting and under-recording of certain crimes – most notably, domestic violence, sexual assaults and racial harassment. Those who are victims of such offences are often **hidden**, both from the official recorded crime statistics and from victimisation surveys. A crucial problem therefore arises if we use victimisation surveys as a guide to the 'risks' of crime for particular social groups.

For example, if, on the basis of BCS findings we reassure women that they are far less likely than their male counterparts to be victims of violent – contact – crime, we may grossly over-simplify (and fail to take seriously) their anxieties about crime. Unreported domestic and acquaintance violence, combined with the specific fears generated by localities (particularly those in areas in 'spirals of decline'), mean that any statistical calculation of risk is problematic. It will not take account of gendered and racialised violence which is hidden, nor will it reflect the genuine fears of potential victims. Put another way, the fears which women and minority ethnic groups have about violent and sexual crimes are related to the **impact** that such appalling crimes have on the lives of the victims, and not the **incidence** or likelihood of it.

Consequently, any assessment of how 'rational' or 'irrational' peoples fears of crime are (in relation to their statistical risk of victimisation) misses the point – the point is that certain individuals, groups and communities will *feel* fearful, and that both their fears and their risks of crime are socially and spatially patterned.

THE 'MYTH OF THE EQUAL VICTIM'

As Young and Lea[13] argue, not all people are equally able to withstand the impact of crime: the theft of £50 will be regarded entirely differently by a pensioner and a well-paid worker. A household burglary will have a different impact on the rich and poor, the insured and uninsured. For the former the 'creative burglary' may offer the opportunity to swap 'old for new' in terms of consumer goods stolen. For the latter it can cause extreme hardship, especially since household insurance is more difficult to obtain and more expensive in those poorer residential areas at 'high risk' of burglary.

The Wolverhampton Poverty Survey found that 25 per cent of all households surveyed were unable to afford the costs of household insurance. But the numbers unable to afford cover rose dramatically for certain groups, notably:

- 53 per cent of those in council rented accommodation;
- 49 per cent of those solely dependent on benefits;
- 42 per cent of Black respondents.[14]

Given such inequities, the poor and their families clearly suffer more than their richer counterparts from this type of crime.

We should not ignore the fact that the impact of victimisation is *qualitative* as well as quantitative: although we have seen that the impact of crime is patterned according to class, 'race', gender, age and locality, not all individuals react in the same ways to the same crimes. Nevertheless, it could be argued that a key factor influencing the ways in which individuals 'recover' from crime is the extent to which they have access to support and redress.

Victim Support is a voluntary service to which all crime victims are referred by the police, in line with the standards set in the Victims Charter (1990).[15] But the Charter's guidelines set the tone of what can be seen as a selective set of rights and expectations when it states that:

> The *majority* of victims are not to blame. *They* deserve to be treated with sympathy and support. (emphasis added)

The policy and practice of supporting and compensating victims is based on the concept of **the deserving victim**. So, who is *not* deserving of sympathy or support? The following press item describes an apparently 'undeserving' case:

> Christina Doolan was working late the night she was robbed and raped. She was hit over the head with a bottle and dragged into bushes where she was forced into oral sex and intercourse. One might think she surely deserves criminal compensation. After all, she had severe cuts and still suffers dizzy spells and panic attacks. She is too frightened to stay in on her own.[16]

Her attacker pleaded guilty and was sentenced to four years' imprisonment, and there was no doubting she was the victim of an extremely serious crime. But Christina was working as a prostitute at the time of the attack, and so the Criminal Injuries Compensation Board (CICB) denied her claim. The 'new' statutory compensation scheme introduced in November 1995 (replacing the previous common law damages scheme), reserved the right to refuse or reduce compensation because of the '**character or conduct**' of the applicant. This echoes the **victim-blaming** so evident in many rape trials. For example, Judge Melford Stevenson (in 1982) commented that a young hitchhiker who was raped was 'in the true sense, asking for it' by her imprudent behaviour. In an equally infamous judgment, Judge Stanforth (in 1993) commented that an eight-year-old victim of rape 'was no angel'.

The CICB scheme resonates with similarly value-laden judgements about the desert and character of crime victims. As the Penal Affairs Consortium notes, there have been cases where the mere fact that the applicant had been drinking alcohol was regarded as a factor in refusal of compensation, even though there was no evidence that this had directly contributed to the incident in any way.[17] Where the victim of crime has a criminal record this too may lead to refusal of criminal injuries compensation. This inevitably begs the question:

> Why should a man or woman given a prison sentence for a non-violent offence who is later violently attacked or raped be denied compensation, or see it substantially reduced, because of unrelated offences for which they have already paid the penalty by serving the sentence?[18]

This also adds a new element to the notion of 'paying for crime' – paying twice. It is a disadvantage which the relatively rich are unlikely to suffer, not least because (as Chapter 4 demonstrated) they are least likely to be processed through the criminal justice system in the first place. However, they are also better able to access the civil courts to obtain redress: recent research indicates that small claims courts are dominated by middle-class individuals, and those on low incomes have poorer access to civil – as well as criminal – justice.[19]

Issues of knowledge, power and the ability to protect oneself against crime are bound to soften the blow of crime for the relatively rich. They invariably have the money, the access to appropriate advice and hence the power to insist on their rights, and to obtain redress for the crimes commited against them.

NOTES

1   J Young and J Lea, *What's To Be Done About Law and Order?*, Pluto Press, 1993.

2   C Mirrlees-Black, P Mayhew and A Percy, *The 1996 British Crime Survey, England and Wales*, Home Office Statistical Bulletin 19/96, Home Office, 1996, p27.

3   S Hall *et al*, *Policing the Crisis*, Macmillan, 1978; P Stubbs, 'Crime, community and the multi-agency approach', in *Critical Social Policy*, Issue 20, Vol 7, No 2, Autumn 1987.

4   *Wolverhampton Council Poverty Study*, Wolverhampton Business School, University of Wolverhampton, Wolverhampton Metropolitan Borough Council, 1996.

5   *Living With More or Less in Wolverhampton*, Wolverhampton MBC Policy and Review Team, Wolverhampton Metropolitan Borough Council, 1996.

6   D Cook and M Roberts, *Wolverhampton Crime Audit 1994-6*, Wolverhampton Community Safety Partnership, 1996, paras 9.1-4.

7   M Coombes, S Raybould, C Wong and S Openshaw, 'Towards an index of deprivation', in *1991 Deprivation Index: a review of approaches and matrix of results*, Department of the Environment, HMSO, 1995.

8   Cook and Roberts, *see* note 6.

9   M Hough, *Anxiety About Crime: findings from the 1994 British Crime Survey*, Home Office Research Study 147, HMSO, 1995.

10   Mirrlees-Black, Mayhew and Percy, *see* note 2, p8.

11   Wolverhampton MBC, *see* note 5.

12   Hough, *see* note 9, p47.

13   Young and Lea, *see* note 1.

14   *Wolverhampton Council Poverty Study*, *see* note 4, p33.

15   Victims Charter, 1990, p8.

16   *Guardian*, 2 November 1995.

17   Penal Affairs Consortium, *Compensation for the Victims of Violence*, PAC, 1994, p7.

18   *Ibid.*

19   *Journal of Social Policy*, July 1996, p403.

7 Social policy, crime and punishment

INTRODUCTION

The Labour Party's landslide victory in the 1997 general election has brought with it the prospect, or at least the hope, of positive social changes. Any fundamental social change must address how criminal justice and social justice are to be reconciled as we enter the 21st century. As David Rose argued, the new government will have to make a crucial decision:

> ... whether it wishes merely to inherit the enhanced powers of the pre-modern criminal justice system and State, or dismantle them and replace them with more humane and democratic institutions ... The door is open to a new settlement between the State and the citizen. The institutions of policing, the law, the courts and the prisons will never be a means of restoring an equitable society. But at the same time, in the absence of *criminal* justice, social justice will remain an unattainable goal.[1] (emphasis in original)

It is (as already argued in Chapter 4) impossible to separate out **criminal** justice from broader issues of **social** justice. Crime and punishment take place in a historical, political and social context and cannot be written off by reference to abstract or legalistic notions of 'justice'.

What I would term 'justice' is therefore a two-way street.[2] Being a law-abiding citizen is part of a two-way contract with the State – this is the essence of the 'settlement' which Rose sees as a precursor for a more humane and democratic society. It follows that if, as a society, we expect people to obey the law, and respect the rights and the property of others, then we should demonstrably provide them with:

- laws which protect people equally;
- laws which are equitably applied;
- penalties for lawbreaking which are both justified and appropriate;
- penalties which are equitably applied to all.

From this brief list we can see that a law abiding society requires a criminal justice system which is seen to be just and fair – if we are to obey the rules of society, both those rules and their implementation must be seen as legitimate. **Legitimacy** depends on the material issues of social justice as well as the philosophical issues of law – as argued earlier, we do, after all, punish *people* and not crimes. In this way, criminal and social justice are interconnected, as are the policies which shape them.

This chapter will examine these connections by focusing on three aspects of the relationship between social policy and criminal justice:

- first, the extent to which the impact of recent social policies on people has led to an erosion of their sense of the **legitimacy**, of the State in general, and the criminal justice system in particular;
- secondly, at a time when the notion of a '**stakeholder society**' is in vogue, we should reflect on how much of a 'stake' certain groups actually have in society, and to what extent their investment is being undermined by the contradictory effects of social policies;
- following on from this and thirdly, the extent to which social policies may have **perverse effects**, in making both crime and punishment *more likely* for vulnerable individuals and social groups.

These issues will be addressed through an analysis of the impact of different social policies on four vulnerable social groups:

- immigration policy and the policing of visible minorities;
- single parent families;
- 'problem' youth;
- the homeless and beggars – 'zero tolerance'?

IMMIGRATION POLICY AND THE POLICING OF VISIBLE MINORITIES

As argued in Chapter 5, moral panics over 'bogus asylum-seekers' and 'illegal immigrants' have connected the issues of race, immigration and benefit fraud in the public mind. As a result, all visible minorities are more likely to be regarded as both suspicious citizens and potential 'scroungers' (particularly following the 1996 Asylum and Immigration Act – discussed in detail below).

The connection between immigration and welfare has long been seen as a direct one by advocates of tougher immigration policies who have, for over half a century, argued that generous welfare benefits act as a '**honeypot**', attracting immigrants who then live off the (over-generous) State. It is most significant that when the then Asylum and Immigration Bill was first announced at the Conservative Party conference in 1995, its proposals were central not only to the speech of Home Secretary Michael Howard, but also to that of the Secretary of State for Social Security, Peter Lilley. Echoing this 'honeypot view', Peter Lilley lamented that:

> The trouble is our system almost invites people to claim asylum to claim British benefits.

In a similar vein, Michael Howard stated that:

> We are seen as a very attractive destination because of the ease with which people can gain access to jobs and benefits ... Only a tiny proportion [of asylum-seekers] are genuine refugees.[3]

By contrast, the United Nations High Commissioner for Refugees issued a ministerial briefing which refuted the view that most claims were bogus and that Britain was a 'soft touch'. Rather, it argued, the rise in asylum claims was the result of 'the unprecedented scale of global conflict which produces refugee flows'.[4]

The aims of cost-cutting, while at the same time demonstrating that 'something is being done', lie at the heart of both immigration and social security policies. The fusion of these two policy areas is evident in the case of the Asylum and Immigration Act. Its provisions include withdrawing asylum-seekers' rights to income support, child benefit and public housing which, the Treasury estimated, would 'save' £200 million. However, local authorities are, in practice, footing the bill because of their statutory duties under the Children Act to feed, clothe and shelter the children of asylum-seekers.[5] Arguably, therefore, the Act is more about deterrence and racial politics than about cash savings.

The implementation of the 1996 Act put into practice the following principles:

- the '**fast tracking**' of appeals, to effectively 'slam the door closed' quicker;

- the judgement of asylum cases not on their individual merits, but on general criteria, including the notorious **'white list'**★ which names the countries from which *all* asylum applications will be presumed to be bogus;
- the **withdrawal of social security**, housing rights from asylum-seekers;
- anyone who does not satisfy entry clearance requirements is liable to **detention** – the decision on detention and bail being taken by Home Office Immigration and Nationality Department (IND) officials;
- applicants may suffer **detention without limit of time** if it is considered that they 'would not meet the conditions attached to remaining at liberty' (although there is no official definition of what this phrase means!);
- restrictions on asylum applications, effected under the **Carriers Liability Act** (whereby airlines and shipping companies are liable to fines if they fail to ensure passengers have visas before embarking).[6]

According to the National Association for the Care and Resettlement of Offenders, the result of these provisions is that:

> The Immigration and Nationality Department possesses and exercises powers which are much more familiar to the criminal justice system and are not found elsewhere within the civil jurisdiction.[7]

Moreover, due to pressure of numbers on limited accommodation, asylum detainees and **suspected immigration 'offenders'** may be held in police cells, prison establishments or in immigration service accommodation which the National Audit Office acknowledged was 'of a poor standard'.[8] These material conditions

---

★ The 'white list' names countries which, according to the then Home Secretary, Michael Howard, have 'no serious risk of general persecution', as they possess:

> functioning institutions, stability and pluralism in sufficient measure to support an assessment that in general people living there are not at risk.

At the time of the Bill's drafting, the white list included Zaire and Nigeria, both countries under oppressive military rule. The execution of activist Ken Saro-Wiwa in Nigeria (within weeks of the white list announcement) and subsequent political turmoil in Zaire, are testimony to the failure of the Home Office's judgement on what constitutes 'stability and pluralism' and lack of personal risk, and to the problems inherent in moving away from an individually based assessment of asylum applications.

themselves mirror the blurring of boundaries between **the suspect citizen** and **the criminal**: the pejorative use of the terms 'suspect' and 'offender' in itself enables and reinforces the criminalization of immigration and asylum issues.

Nonetheless, both Michael Howard and Peter Lilley emphasised that '**deserving**' asylum and immigration applicants had 'nothing to fear' from their new proposals, a reassurance which has been rendered hollow – not only because of the deterrent character of the regulations themselves, and the appalling physical conditions that these civil prisoners suffer – but because of the suspicion, fear and stress which *all* visible minorities are increasingly likely to suffer as a result of this legislation.

The Commission for Racial Equality described the Bill as having an 'anti-black and xenophobic message', a message which will permeate the lives of all 'visible' ethnic minorities in Britain, regardless of their formal citizenship status. The level of policing which is both *encouraged and enabled* by the Act will particularly affect families as they interact with a variety of social, legal and welfare agencies. The dubious practice of passport checking where individuals 'appear to be foreign' has long rendered the citizenship rights of Black people in Britain **questionable**.[9] But under the Act this practice will be developed as headteachers, hospital administrators, housing and social security staff are trained and encouraged to identify and report suspected illegal immigrants. Similarly, employers are required to confirm workers' immigration status and may be fined up to £5,000 for hiring illegal immigrant labour (despite the protests of employers' groups that this proposal could lead to discrimination).

The role of employers and social welfare agencies in 'snooping' adds another dimension to the existing policing (official and unofficial) of visible minorities: for example, in 1993 around 60 per cent of cases of 'suspected immigration offenders' were referred to the Home Office by the police and by anonymous 'tip-offs' from the public (although, significantly, three-quarters of these were found to be groundless).[10] The Asylum and Immigration Act, dubbed a 'snoopers' charter', can only add to this climate of fear and suspicion surrounding all minority ethnic groups, which will find expression in the routine policing of families in schools, hospitals, housing and social security offices and at work.

It is worth emphasising that the fundamental change which the Act has signalled towards 'social policing' has been supported by the new approach to 'data matching' and **inter-departmental**

co-operation introduced by the former (Conservative) government.[11] Routine practice on information disclosure *between* departments has been radically changed to accommodate the objectives of the Act.

Previously, the exchange of information between departments was tightly regulated: as far as the Benefits Agency was concerned, with the exception of the Employment Services Agency (which acted as an agent of the Benefits Agency in paying income support – and now also jobseeker's allowance – to unemployed customers), there were 'very few occasions when information [was] passed on to other departments'. However, a *Memorandum of Understanding* between the Benefits Agency and the Immigration and Nationality Department was signed in October 1995 in anticipation of the implementation of the Act. It allows for an unprecedented level of information to pass between the two departments – notably, information can be shared if the individual is a '**known or suspected immigration offender**'.[12]

In summary, I would argue that the Asylum and Immigration Act enables a new and covert form of 'sus' law which signals a worrying blurring of the boundaries between the jurisdictions of the civil and criminal law. Asylum applicants who have broken no criminal law may nonetheless be incarcerated in penal institutions – a fact emphasised by the recent protests and hunger strikes of detainees in Rochester Prison. But more generally, this fusion of immigration, welfare and criminal law has wider social implications: I have already argued that minority ethnic communities are liable to disproportionate **formal policing** (Chapter 4). Immigration legislation has added another dimension – by enabling the intensified **social policing** of visible minority ethnic families, groups and communities in Britain.

LONE PARENT FAMILIES

In a speech to the National Children's Home (NCH) in 1990, Margaret Thatcher spoke of the threat that lone parents posed 'to our whole way of life' and stressed the right of children to belong to a '*real* family' – one with two parents, still together. The notion of the nuclear family based on the breadwinner-husband/dependant-wife relationship has formed the basis of post-war welfare provision. The Beveridge report clearly distinguished the single and the married woman, the latter being seen to belong in the home, bearing children and so

> ensuring the continuance of the British race and British ideals in the world.[13]

The modern British welfare state is still based on this ideal-type nuclear family, which no longer corresponds with the reality of alternative family forms and the lived experience of increasing numbers of women. As Table 7.1 indicates, the *number* of lone parent families has increased dramatically – almost doubling over the last ten years. The *proportion* of lone parents dependent on income support has (with the exception of 1992-3) remained fairly constant, indicating that the welfare costs of lone parenthood have risen more because of the increasing incidence of single parent families than because of any increasing levels of welfare dependency.

TABLE 7.1: **Number of income support lone parents**

Year	No of cases	% of lone parent population
1986	595,000	62
1987	629,000	64
1988	694,000	66
1989	756,000	67
1990	871,000	65
1991	957,000	66
1992	957,000	68
1993	1,013,000	68
1994	1,039,000	66
1995	1,056,000	64

Source: *Benefits*, January, 1997, p36.

The period 1992/93 marked a sustained political and media moral panic over 'single mums'. Although (as Chapter 5 demonstrated) lone mothers have long been targeted as 'fraud prone', the furore of 1992/93 elevated the single mum to new heights within the scrounger mythology. She (and the 'errant father' of her children) figured prominently in Peter Lilley's rhyming list of '**benefit offenders**', which drew laughter and much applause from the 1992 Conservative Party conference audience:

> Young ladies who get pregnant just to jump the housing list
> And Dads who won't support the kids of ladies they have ... kissed.[14]

Evidence of queue-jumping mothers was (anecdotally) provided by the now infamous Panorama programme *Babies on Benefit*, which served to confirm the very worst aspects of this particular stereotype.

The same was true of a *Sunday Times* cartoon (11 July 1993) captioned 'Sugar Daddy', used to illustrate a 'four-page special report' entitled *Wedded to Welfare – Do they Want to Marry a Man or the State?* Despite well-evidenced rebuttals from housing associations and the National Council for One Parent Families, the myth took hold – that there were vast numbers of 'teenage mums' getting pregnant deliberately in order to obtain welfare benefits and council housing.

Aspiring Conservative Party leader and Welsh Secretary, John Redwood, provided much of the ammunition for the *Sunday Times* article in his recollections of a visit to the St Mellons Estate, Cardiff where:

> six in ten children belong to unmarried mothers and crime is rife.

Illegitimacy and crime are seen as both inseparable and causal features of life on this 'sink' estate. Directly invoking the concept of the underclass, the article summarises the concerns of both Redwood and Lilley as follows:

> They believe the country is at risk in more than financial ways from
> the spiralling of illegitimate births and the rising numbers of unmarried
> mothers dependent on welfare benefits. On the St Mellons estate,
> and scores like it, the underclass has not only arrived: it dominates.[15]

The cartoon offered us a visual version of this moral tale because, in an instant, we could 'read' the following:

> *The **single mother** – with three children already – is pregnant yet again.*
> *She is nonetheless marrying (in white) the faceless social security system – a*
> *dupe who is, literally, 'full' of money. Meanwhile, her partner, the **errant***
> ***father**, remains deliberately in the background, drinking (presumably) a can*
> *of lager. His lack of family responsibility is denoted by his tattoo, which*
> *proclaims 'free love'.*
> *The **locality** in which the tale unfolds is a **crime-prone estate***
> *characterised by high rise flats, burned out cars and motorbikes. The*
> ***children** resemble their parents – boys with shaven haircuts, and a girl with*

This cartoon was used to illustrate a Sunday Times *special report:*
'Wedded to Welfare — Do They Want to Marry a Man or the State?'
© *Cole*/The Sunday Times, *11 July 1993*

her mother's lascivious leer: we presume they will turn out just like Mum and Dad, and so perpetuate the demoralised **underclass**.

This imagery remains ideologically powerful and its underlying assumptions remain intact. Current social policies continue to put a premium on marriage and the traditional nuclear family. For example, the 1996 Budget introduced changes

to bring the structure of benefits for lone parents *into line* with that for couples.[16] (my emphasis)

In practice, from April 1997, lone parent benefit has been integrated with child benefit, and the lone parent premium will be combined with the family premium. These measures effectively *cut* benefits for lone parents under the guise of 'equalising' their status with that of couples.[17] Higher one-parent benefits are effectively scrapped for all new claims from April 1998. Such policies confirm Will Hutton's interpretation — that the government regards the only deserving poor as 'those in work and in good nuclear families'.[18]

The 'premium on marriage' which dates from the 1942 Beveridge report was still evident in the tax proposals announced in the 1997 Conservative Party manifesto. This policy favoured *two* tax allowances for *married* couples with children, where only one of the couple is working. This would not apply to cohabiting couples because, as then Prime Minister John Major confirmed, he was 'in favour' of marriage. The Labour manifesto placed the family 'at the core of our society' and pledged a childcare strategy to:

match the requirements of the modern labour market and help parents, especially women, to balance family and working life.

But this balance is not an easy one to strike: to ensure family (and thereby social) stability it is not enough to be married and not enough to be working either, because we are told that:

Women who juggle a full-time job with motherhood may jeopardise their children's future. (Panorama: *Missing Mum*, February 1997)

So, in the 'real' family, Mum must not only be married to Dad, and living with him, she must *not* be working full time! It is difficult to see how this paradox can be resolved within the terms of New Labour's new childcare strategy. Although a 'coherent programme for the education and care of young children' has been promised by the new government, the first example of their putting this programme into practice has been by launching 'after school clubs at which children can do their homework' (Tony Blair, speech at Aylesbury Estate, Southwark, 2 June 1997). These American-style clubs, to be funded by lottery cash, hardly constitute an adequate response to the needs of working mothers for appropriate, accessible and affordable childcare. It certainly falls far short of the measures needed to fulfil Blair's aim to 'empower' single mothers in the labour market.

Lone mothers are seen to jeopardise their children's future in very fundamental ways, and their failure is accentuated, not mitigated, by their poverty – as they are seen as to **blame** for that poverty:

> Recourse to wider social factors such as poverty only extenuates the process of blaming: a single mother's children may turn out to be criminals because of living in poverty as children. But if *she* chooses to bring them up in poverty (by rejecting the possibility of bringing them up with two parents) then she can be blamed ... for their later criminality.[19]

Despite the recent change of government, there has been little change in the ways in which the links between lone mothers, poverty and, ultimately, criminality are conceptualised.

> For part of a generation of young women early pregnancies and the absence of a reliable father almost guarantee a life of poverty.[20]

In the context of New Labour's 'bargain' of mutual responsibility, we are told that 'we play by the rules. You only take out what you put in. That's the bargain.' But in this context, lone mothers are inevitably constituted as 'takers' and not givers in the modern civic society.[21]

The notion of the deserving and undeserving poor still, therefore, underlies how lone parenthood – or, more accurately, lone motherhood – is conceptualised. According to many Conservative commentators (ranging from Sir Keith Joseph to John Redwood), those women who are bringing up children alone through 'no fault of their own' (for instance, widows) are **deserving** of state and social support. But others who have never married, or who have left relationships, are blameworthy and hence **undeserving**. This view of welfare is in line with the ideas of Patrick Minford who, a decade ago, argued that the safety net of state support should not be provided in cases of 'avoidable need' – or 'self-inflicted misfortune':

those who have illegitimate children will suffer; illegitimacy is therefore discouraged.[22]

This discouragement is effected through social policies which have increasingly policed lone mothers on social security (as potential fraudsters) and which, arguably, seek to deter their claiming through cuts in already 'less eligible' levels of benefit.[23] Previous research has indicated how deterrence combines with the 'scrounger' stigma in the ways in which some women are:

> precipitated into relationships they did not want or were at least doubtful about, because of DSS suggestions that they could avoid allegations of fraud if they move in with boyfriends.[24]

Women who do not depend on men may end up depending on the State, and so one solution to their problems (and society's too) is for them to find a man – preferably a husband. One magistrate expressed precisely these sentiments when passing sentence on two young women aged 20 and 22:

> The real hope is that girls like these, presentable girls, is that they'll find a man to take them on, look after them and their children.[25]

In this way, social policy, and some criminal justice professionals, clearly foresee the 'problem' of single motherhood being solved by a game of state-sponsored 'happy families'.

However, those families must stay together, and stay happy. According to the 'criminological concordats' ironically described by Alison Young, not only does divorce predispose children to delinquency, but so does disharmony:

> Marital discord is ... an originating condition for the downward spiral with moral, fiscal and social consequences: the damage done to the status of marriage in society, damage done to the psyche of the child resulting in anti-social behaviour, damage to the community through the perpetration of offences, damage to the nation through the cost of responding to delinquent children.[26]

The burden of keeping the family together and keeping society orderly is placed squarely on mothers. As Young continues:

> To avoid delinquency, parents are thus placed under a duty to provide surveillance, to give love as a surety and to display involvement in their child's activities and interests.

But here 'parent' means mother: it is the responsibility of *women* to ensure the 'next generation of future law-abiding adults. In this respect, the bonds of maternal love become the bonds of disciplinary duty'.[27] So, once again, lone motherhood, poverty and the criminality of youth are seen to be either the product of women's choices or their failures.

'PROBLEM' YOUTH

> It might be wondered what kind of a country it is that chooses to focus on young people in this way ... Little is said of diminishing opportunities for young people (jobs, money, accommodation, a stake in things) and their prospects. The high profile currently enjoyed by crime ... makes it easier to evade responsibility and to deceive the public into believing that the answer is for the courts to 'get tough' if faced with bad behaviour.[28]

The high profile of the youth crime 'problem' can be seen as a diversion from the deep-seated social problems faced by contemporary youth. Its high profile should also be located in the context of deep-seated ideologies about lone parenthood, crime-prone families and the underclass (Chapter 1).

One response to a series of 'moral panics' over juvenile delinquency has been the reassertion of **parental responsibility** for juvenile offending – not just morally but legally. This concept dates from (at least) the Criminal Justice Act 1982 which first established parental responsibility for fines or compensation orders for juveniles.[29] The 1991 Criminal Justice Act introduced the 'bind-over' for parents, enforcing their obligations 'to take proper care of him (sic) and to exercise proper control over him'. A *Times* Leader in 1990 had tellingly commented that:

> This is the kind of proposal that makes perfect sense to middle class ministers, who generally leave the taming of adolescence to their children's boarding schools.[30]

Similarly, an editorial in *The Magistrate* argued that:

> it will not work in terms of preventing further re-offending, but ... is likely to be counter-productive, leading to an increase in family breakdown and hence in already unacceptable levels of homelessness amongst teenagers.[31]

The high profile of the youth crime 'problem' can be seen as a diversion from the deep-seated social problems faced by contemporary youth.

Credit: Paula Solloway/Format

Not only are such youth justice policies doomed to failure, they have negative social consequences too – the likelihood of increased youth homelessness and a deepening of poverty, should already-poor parents be financially penalised for their children's offending.

Arguably, the 1991 Act could, on the whole, be considered forward-looking where youth justice was concerned: it introduced the Youth Court and built upon earlier policies (developed through the 1980s) focusing on the need for multi-agency and community-based approaches to working with young offenders, with the aim of constructively 'challenging' their offending behaviour.[32] But the announcement in May 1992 that sections of the 1991 Act were to be repealed indicated a fundamental U-turn by the then Home Secretary, Kenneth Clarke, on youth justice policy.

Following successive media campaigns – over ram-raiding, joyriding, raves, vandalism and 'bail bandits' – and the murder of Jamie Bulger, ministers reacted in 'knee-jerk' fashion – by being seen to act 'tough' on crime, and tough on youth crime in particular. According to Gibson,[33] criminal justice thereafter became 'heavily politicised'.

The subsequent 1993 Criminal Justice Act and the Criminal Justice and Public Order Act 1994 have both produced higher incarceration rates for young people. They reflect the flawed policy stance that:

> ... locking up more young people at younger ages, for longer periods and in a wider range of custodial settings, will help to reduce youth crime. It was because of the experience and evidence showing this to be the reverse of the truth that policies designed to reduce the unnecessary institutionalisation of young people have been developed over the last twelve years.[34]

Failing to learn from history, the provisions of the 1993 and 1994 Acts included:

- secure training orders for 12–14-year-olds;
- long-term detention for 10–13-year-olds who commit serious offences;
- increases in the maximum length of detention in a young offender institution for 15–17-year-olds from one to two years; *and*
- secure remands in custody for 15 and 16-year-olds.

To take the final example, recent figures show that custodial remands for juveniles rose by 72 per cent between 1992 and 1995, and that the daily number remanded increased fourfold during this period.[35] As Paul Cavadino stresses (see quotation above), all the evidence points to the fact that institutionalising young offenders (or, in the case of custodial remands – young suspects) simply does *not* deter or reduce crime. At a very basic level, it is possible to argue that as so *few* crimes are detected, and so few defendants go to court (see Figure 4.4), to assume that anything we do to offenders (by way of punishment) will have *any* impact on crime rates is simply a nonsense!

Recently opened American-style 'boot camps' for young offenders are further evidence of the political U-turn over youth justice, and also echo earlier attempts (in 1983), to discipline unruly and criminal youth by the '**short, sharp, shock**' method. But in terms of its stated aim (deterring future offending) the short sharp shock was the most clear-cut failure in recent penal history.[36] Rates of re-offending were unaffected, although the young men were released in better physical shape – and more 'fit' to escape the police in future! The same fate may befall the new boot camps.

But criminal justice policy in general (and youth justice in particular) does not have to make sense – it just has to appear to please the public. The Audit Commission's recent report, *Misspent Youth*,[37] persuasively argues that the existing system is inefficient, expensive and fails young people: it fails to guide them away from re-offending and wastes resources **processing** young offenders rather than **working with** them. It is estimated that the criminal justice system spends £1 billion a year on dealing with youth crime – the Audit Commission clearly believes this is not money well spent.

Meanwhile, there is no shortage of media coverage and political rhetoric about the youth crime problem, although there is an apparent lack of both realism and honesty about the outcomes of 'get tough' policies. By contrast, when commenting on boot camps for young offenders, the Chief Inspector of Prisons, Sir David Ramsbotham, candidly responded:

> For the life of me, I can see little point in forming young civilian offenders up in threes and marching them around.[38]

Nor can I.

When it comes to youth crime, both major political parties were vying for public support during the 1997 election campaign in a policy 'Dutch auction' which was reminiscent of the one held around low taxation (see Chapter 5). For example, on the issue of parental responsibility for young offenders, Conservative proposals for 'Parental *Control* Orders' were paralleled by New Labour's 'Parental *Responsibility* Orders'. While a one-word difference did signal an alternative emphasis, the overall congruence of their youth crime policies was remarkable.

In his first major speech as Prime Minister, significantly made at a 'sink' estate in Southwark, Tony Blair highlighted his proposed 'crackdown on crime and other anti-social behaviour'. This was primarily directed at the young:

> Our Youth Offender Teams are going to nip young offending in the bud. Young children wandering the streets at night, getting into trouble, growing into a life of criminality, will be subject to child protection orders. (Tony Blair, 2 June 1997)

But New Labour's plans for curfews for the under-10s received short shrift from some quarters: as one resident of a Bradford estate declared:

> It's the MPs who need an effing curfew after what they and their council's done to us on this estate. I'd like to see them come here.[39]

Despite the apparent emphasis on youth training and employment in recent 'welfare to work' proposals, the main plank of the Labour government's law and order policy remains a commitment to combat youth crime. To return to Bryan Gibson's comment (see p143), the issue of **investment in youth** is one which is largely concealed by political posturing over crime and disorder, and the emphasis on 'get tough' policies which are known to have failed in the recent past. Social investment will entail prioritising and resourcing policies to tackle youth unemployment which is, justifiably, the dominant concern of young people themselves.[40] Recent Labour Force data indicates that:

- 281,000 16–19-year-olds were unemployed during the winter of 1995/96;
- the unemployment rate among young males is the highest of any age group, at 19.6 per cent (recorded, registered unemployment);
- 4 per cent of males and 5 per cent of females aged 16–19 are classed as long-term unemployed – out of work for over a year.[41]

The patterning of poverty and unemployment are paralleled by inequalities in the health of young people, with children in the lowest class ('unskilled manual') households being twice as likely to die before the age of 15 as those in the highest professional groups.

Moreover, unemployment and poverty-related stress may be contributing to an increase in suicide among the young.[42]

Social investment in youth offers a better prospect for both reducing crime and maximising the human capital which the young represent. In relation to preventing and reducing offending, the *National Protocol for Youth Justice Services*, sets this in the context of:

> promoting the best interests of young people, given that this age group is one of the most criticised and *least valued* in society.[43] (emphasis added)

Following on from that view, and building on the notion of *valuing* and acting in the best interests of youth, the Penal Affairs Consortium aptly states that:

> The approach with the best prospect of reducing reoffending is the provision of high quality programmes of education, training, drug treatment, and focused work to change attitudes to crime and tackle offending behaviour.[44]

This is a clear statement of what **social inclusion**, developing a sense of social citizenship, would entail for young people in general, and young offenders in particular. It also echoes what Pat Carlen[45] termed a '**state-obligated rehabilitation**' model of justice, whereby the state acknowledged that it (as well as the offender) had some responsibility for crime and redress. According to this view, the purpose of 'justice' is to ensure that the likelihood of reoffending is reduced by ameliorating the socio-economic conditions which generate (or underlie) much of the offending in the first place.[46] It is at this point that a direct connection between social policy and criminal justice becomes crystal clear.

For young people, as for adults, issues of social policy and criminal justice are inseparable. They deal with the same constituencies and are shaped by the same (contradictory) political ideologies and policies – social policy frequently subverts the intentions of broader criminal justice policies which are geared to preventing crime. The work of Gill Jones evidences this paradox:

> While it may be desirable to construct youth as a period of dependency on parents rather than the state, this is in theory at least achieving the twin goals of *reducing the social security budget* and *increasing law and order*, there are various reasons why this policy cannot work ... dependency is problematic, it is associated with resistance rather than

social control, and power relations in the family can also be complex. Furthermore, it becomes increasingly untenable for rhetoric to stress citizenship responsibilities on the one hand, and withdraw them from young people on the other.[47] (emphasis added)

The issue of parental responsibility is clearly a case in point – where the young are encouraged to take courses in citizenship, but their civil responsibility is in practice denied. On the problem of dependency and family tension:

> At present, education, training and social security policies appear to be based on the assumptions that young people can remain dependent on their parents beyond the age of 16, that parents will take up the slack when social security is withdrawn and that parent-child relations can be regulated to ensure that this occurs.[48]

For the parents of over three million dependent children currently living on income support, the notion of any 'slack' in the family income is patently ludicrous. The fact that 16–18-year-olds are not entitled to social security (now jobseeker's allowance) merely turns the screw of poverty for the most disadvantaged families. The possible impact of such policy contradictions, in terms of family breakdown and the potential for youth crime, is clear – particularly for the young homeless whose parents cannot afford to take up the slack from the welfare state, or who are seen to have 'failed' to live amicably at home.

THE HOMELESS AND BEGGARS: ZERO TOLERANCE?

> We think aggressive begging is a menace. Action has been taken against aggressive begging for some time and it will continue. (Prime Minister John Major, 28 May 1994)

> There are the obstacles faced by pedestrians and motorists in going about their daily business. The winos and addicts whose aggressive begging affronts and sometimes threatens decent, compassionate citizens. And the 'squeegee merchants' who wait at large road junctions to force on reticent motorists their wind-screen cleaning services. (Jack Straw, Shadow Home Secretary quoted in *Independent on Sunday*, 10 September 1995)

In spite of party political differences, it appears that, for some, the homeless beggar presents a threat to all 'decent' citizens.

The growing gap between rich and poor (documented in Chapter 2) has been accompanied by visual evidence of that gap on our streets: the homeless, mentally ill, prostitutes and beggars all testimony to a society where poverty is a fact of life, however uncomfortable. Politicians from left and right appear to have adopted wholesale the New York policy of 'zero tolerance' in their strategies to deal with the physical and criminal nuisance which these groups are seen to present.

The policy rests on the assumption that a clampdown on *all* crimes, no matter how trivial, will eventually lead to a reduction in more serious crime. The reduction in the murder rate in New York is widely lauded as the positive outcome of zero tolerance policing (of graffiti, drinking in public places and street crime). However, some senior English police officers doubt the claims made: for example, Charles Pollard (Chief Constable of the Thames Valley force) pointedly reminds us that an extra 7,000 officers on top of an already high ratio of police to public may have had a great deal to do with the success in reducing the New York homicide rate.[49]

A critical perspective on zero tolerance is also offered by criminologist Rod Morgan:

> Zero tolerance is all about sweeping clean those inner city junctions where tourists and commuters briefly encounter the dispossessed underclass – the mad and the sad as well as the bad. Kings Cross is not so much dangerous as socially uncomfortable.[50]

The metaphor of moral and physical hygiene is also clear in the way in which zero tolerance policing was hailed as a success in the winter 1996 'clean-up' of Kings Cross. But critics argue that such strategies merely push the problem elsewhere – the result is not a solution but a displacement, of both people and problems. Moreover, Charles Pollard, who was formerly of the Metropolitan police, warned that its effects could be counter-productive:

> The problem is that sustained policing of this sort ends up targeting minorities within communities ... That was the case in Brixton in 1981 during Operation Swamp, which could be described as 'zero tolerance'.[51]

This raises the question of whether this strategy tolerates 'zero' crimes on the part of *all* citizens, at all times, in all places. The answer is 'no'. Clearly it is the crimes of the poorest (and dispossessed) groups which are defined as the 'crime problem' that needs to be tackled, and to which resources are allocated (see Chapter 3). It is significant that when advocating action to deter the anti-social behaviour resulting from drinking in public places, the then Shadow Home Secretary, Jack Straw, reassured journalists that:

> Your picnic with claret by the banks of the Thames will be safe in Labour's hands.[52]

But, presumably, a can of lager in the hands of a beggar in Kings Cross will not be. Put simply, zero tolerance is not a policy applied to the crimes of the respectable or the rich – it is directed only to **vulnerable** and **visible** targets.

Arguably, these visible problems of homelessness, poverty and petty crime are a logical product of the social and fiscal policies of the 1980s and '90s.[53] For example, the sale of council housing, restrictions on local government spending, restrictions on benefit entitlement for young people and 'community care' policies in relation to the mentally ill have all had a knock on effect in deepening the poverty and vulnerability of these groups.

The 1996 (Conservative) Budget only exacerbated these problems. For instance, in relation to housing, measures included restricting housing benefit for single tenants to the cost of one person renting one room in a shared home, and limiting all private tenants to housing benefit equivalent to the average rent of a 'suitable' sized home. Secretary of State Peter Lilley justified this action in terms of cutting costs to the taxpayer, and encouraging more financial responsibility amongst benefit claimants. It was argued that:

> Both changes will encourage people on benefit to take cost into account in deciding where to live, and they will have the choice of paying from their own incomes for more expensive accommodation, or trying to negotiate their rent downwards, or moving to a home they and the taxpayer can afford.[54]

The notion that benefit claimants had the advantage of either 'income' or a 'choice' in relation to securing their housing, or the scope for 'negotiating their rent downwards' was clearly absurd. But the social consequences of such policies, coupled with the legacy of a diminished council housing stock, were alarming:

> As the supply of social housing dries up, homelessness and social

distress will rise. The acute social conditions at the bottom of society that incubate disease, criminality and the collapse of self-worth are set to become more acute still.[55]

This indicates the compounding effects of poverty and deprivation. Here, disease does not equate with the eighteenth century metaphor for crime, although criminality is envisaged as one by-product of these social conditions. Disease may better refer to the range of physical and mental conditions – from low birth weight, respiratory illness, heart disease and strokes to depression and mental illness – which disproportionately blight the lives of the poorest social groups.[56]

When zero tolerance policies are applied to groups who suffer such impoverished circumstances, all that is accomplished is the displacement of their physical presence and the denial of their very existence. These policies are currently espoused by the new Labour government, which is simultaneously committed to reducing inequality. It remains to be seen whether it is possible for this government to reconcile their rhetoric of zero tolerance with their overarching commitment to social justice.

SUMMARY

To return to the questions posed at the beginning of this chapter, first, I would argue that the cumulative effect of the social policies described here has, over the past two decades, been to erode any faith which minority ethnic families and communties, lone mothers, young people and the homeless may have in the (welfare) State and the criminal justice system. As senior police officers are beginning to publicly assert, if a sense of **legitimacy** is lacking for these groups, then this may ultimately pose problems of social order as well as justice.

Secondly, if being law-abiding partly rests on having a **stake in society**, then social policies which impoverish and/or disempower these groups will only serve to 'push' them towards law-breaking – what, after all, do they have to lose? As Hudson succinctly observes, 'people give up crime when they acquire bonds to the social order'.[57]

Thirdly, social policies may have perverse and **contradictory effects** which make crime more, not less, likely. The impoverishing effects of welfare benefit cuts on lone mothers, the withdrawal of social security benefits for young people, punitive deductions (for voluntary unemployment) from jobseeker's allowance and the long-term effects of housing policies may all play a part in pushing some individuals with ever-narrowing options towards crimes of poverty.

Moreover, irrespective of whether they actually commit crime, the poverty, stigma and targeting of these groups makes it more likely that their behaviour will be policed and criminalised.

NOTES

1 D Rose, *In the Name of the Law*, Jonathan Cape, 1996, p336.
2 J Reiman, *The Rich Get Richer and the Poor Get Prison*, Macmillan, 1990.
3 *Guardian*, 26 October 1995.
4 UNHCR, 13 January 1996.
5 *Poverty*, CPAG Ltd, Spring 1997.
6 NACRO *Race Policies into Action*, Spring 1997.
7 *Ibid*, p3.
8 National Audit Office, *Entry in the United Kingdom*, HC204, HMSO, 1995, p71.
9 D Cook, 'Racism, citizenship and exclusion', in D Cook and B Hudson (eds), *Racism and Criminology*, Sage, 1993.
10 National Audit Office, *see* note 8.
11 D Cook, 'Official secrecy and social policy research', in H Dean (ed), *Ethics and Social Policy Research*, SPA/University of Luton Press, 1996.
12 *Ibid*.
13 *Social Insurance and Allied Services*, Cmd 6404, HMSO, 1942, p52.
14 *Daily Mirror*, 8 October 1992.
15 *Sunday Times*, 11 July 1993.
16 DSS Press Release, 26 November 1996.
17 *Ibid*.
18 *Observer*, 1 December 1996.
19 A Young, *Imagining Crime: textual outlaws and criminal conversations*, Sage, 1996, p163.
20 *Ibid*.
21 *Ibid*.
22 P Minford, 'The role of the social services: the view from the Right', in M Loney (ed), *The State or the Market*, Sage, 1987, p81.
23 C Oppenheim and L Harker, *Poverty: the facts*, CPAG Ltd, 1996.
24 Welfare rights worker, quoted in D Cook, 'Social Disadvantage and Offending', unpublished paper to NAPO Bail Hostels Conference, UMIST, Manchester, September 1991.

25 H Parker, M Sumner and G Jarvis, *Unmasking the Magistrates*, Open University Press, 1989, p77.
26 A Young, *Imagining Crime: textual outlaws and criminal conversations*, Sage, 1996, p173.
27 *Ibid*, p154.
28 B Gibson, 'Young people, bad news, enduring principles', in *Youth and Policy*, Issue 48, Spring 1995, p64.
29 Penal Affairs Consortium, *Parental Responsibility, Youth Crime and the Criminal Law*, PAC, 1995.
30 *The Times*, 10 November 1990.
31 *The Magistrate*, January 1991.
32 *Ibid*.
33 Gibson, *see* note 28.
34 P Cavadino, 'The Criminal Justice and Public Order Act and young offenders', in *Youth and Policy*, Issue 48, Spring 1995, p83.
35 Penal Affairs Consortium, *Juveniles on Remand*, PAC, 1996.
36 Penal Affairs Consortium, *Boot Camps for Young Offenders*, PAC, 1995.
37 Audit Commission, *Misspent Youth: young people and crime*, Audit Commission, 1996.
38 NACRO *Digest*, February 1997.
39 *Guardian*, 23 June 1996.
40 A Dennehey, L Smith and P Harker, *Not To Be Ignored: young people, poverty and health*, CPAG Ltd, 1997, p24.
41 *Ibid*, p16.
42 *Ibid*.
43 *National Protocol for Youth Justice Services*, 1996.
44 PAC, *see* note 36.
45 P Carlen, 'Crime, inequality and sentencing', in P Carlen and D Cook (eds), *Paying for Crime*, Open University Press, 1989.
46 *Ibid*.
47 G Jones and C Wallace, *Youth, Family and Citizenship*, Open University Press, 1992, pp154-5.
48 G Jones, *Family Policy Bulletin*, September 1994.
49 *Guardian*, 10 April 1997.
50 *Guardian*, 22 January 1997.
51 *Guardian*, 10 April 1997.
52 *Guardian*, 26 April 1996.
53 A Walker and C Walker (eds), *Britain Divided: the growth of social exclusion in the 1980s and 1990s*, CPAG Ltd, 1997.
54 DSS Press Release, 26 November 1996.
55 Will Hutton, *Observer*, 1 December 1996.
56 Dennehy, Smith and Harker, *see* note 40.
57 B Hudson, *Justice Through Punishment*, Macmillan, 1987.

8 Conclusions

CRIME: WHO SUFFERS?

Despite the problems of defining and measuring crime (described in Chapter 3), it seems probable that crime – as measured by official statistics and victimisation surveys – has increased dramatically since 1980. At the same time, poverty and social inequality have increased. I would argue that we therefore need to face up to the **failures of recent criminal justice and social policies** which, over the same period, have combined to:

- **widen the gap** between rich and poor (Chapters 2 and 7);
- **reinforce and magnify** social inequalities along lines of age, gender and 'race' (Chapters 2, 3, 4, 6 and 7);
- increase the **vulnerability** of the poorest individuals, families and communities to criminal **victimisation** (Chapter 6);
- make the commission of crime by both the rich and the poor **more likely** (albeit for different reasons, and under different circumstances – Chapters 3, 4 and 5);
- **intensify** the policing, regulation, criminalisation and punishment of poorer individuals, families and communities (Chapters 1, 3, 4, 5 and 7).

CRIME: WHO BENEFITS?

I have termed these outcomes 'failures' – but if we adopt Reiman's somewhat ironic argument),[1] these penal and social policies could be seen as *successful* on at least three counts:

- **first**, the blame for crime, disorder and moral decline can all be placed squarely on the poor – the underclass – which leaves the 'overclass' with a sense of civic and moral virtue;
- **secondly**, the booming criminal justice and security industries generate both jobs and profits; while
- **thirdly**, anti-crime rhetoric is believed to generate votes for politicians and simultaneously provides food for a hungry media.

DE-MORALISATION

We also need to face up to the disturbing implications of **'failed' criminal justice policies** in order to identify:

- their underlying assumptions about the causes of, and hence the cures for, crime; *and*
- the essentially ideological roots from which these assumptions have grown.

An illustration of this process is provided by Rose[2] who quotes at length from a *Sunday Times* article by a columnist, and wife of a 'media magnate', in which she puts forward her explanations for, and solution to, the problem of crime. Both are predicated on the (alleged) **moral hazards** which I have described at length elsewhere in this book:

- the decline in the nuclear family;
- the permissive society and single parenthood;
- a cosseting welfare state (coupled with high rates of personal taxation);
- the perils of the underclass;
- social de-moralisation;
- the politics of envy (egalitarianism);
- and, of course, immigration.

This one extract uncomfortably displays all of these themes in a particularly sinister fashion:

> From the 1960s on, the family was seen as too restrictive. We whittled away at its authority, made a two-parent family with a stay-at-home mother a fiscal liability through tax policies, created the conditions for children to parent children (by removing taboos on teenage sex) ... In effect, we subsidised and financed an enlarged

underclass, pooh-poohed the bootstrap mentality of the poor ... described the bettering of oneself as yuppie behaviour or greed, and promoted envy as common currency. Together with unrestricted immigration policies from Asian and African countries at levels too high to allow for assimilation, we allowed the nightmares of Enoch Powell to come true (though without the blood on the streets) ... In summary: we cannot deport people who are now here. But we can segregate the underclass and forget about egalitarian principles. We should try to reintroduce the best of our principles while getting rid of the worst. We must stop ruining our free society by enacting rules appropriate for a zoo. Just because some of the rooms in the house have been taken over by pigs and donkeys does not mean we should turn the entire kingdom into a place for the housing of animals.[3]

The 'animal' analogy clearly signifies the fascist tone of the extract which denies the 'underclass' (and minority ethnic groups in particular) their dignity, humanity and intelligence. Nevertheless, her main suggestions – to abandon egalitarianism and segregate the poorest individuals and groups – are already well under way. In practice – the realities of **social exclusion, sink estates and zero tolerance** are testimony to that.

POVERTY, CRIME AND PUNISHMENT – COMPLICATING THE PICTURE

I have argued that the relationship between poverty, crime and punishment is far more complex than many politicians and most popular mythologies would have us believe. This relationship has most frequently been seen in terms of a two-step argument of cause and effect: **poverty causes crime; crime leads to punishment** (see Model 1 in Figure 8.1).

But I have argued that both steps in this argument are flawed:

- first, while poverty may be a key **source** of crime it is an insufficient **explanation** for it – not least because much crime is committed by non-poor individuals and wealthy corporations;
- secondly, the case of white-collar crime demonstrates that **not all crimes lead to punishment**;
- thirdly, **not all punishment is the result of crime**, as the asylum detainees in Rochester Prison can testify. Moreover, there

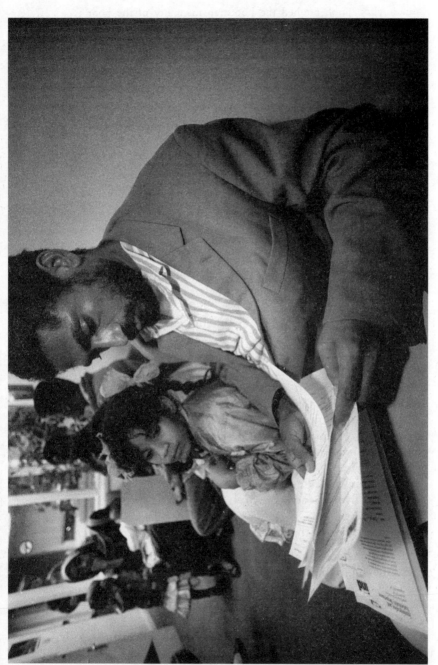

Immigration legislation has enabled the intensified social policing of visible minority ethnic families, groups and communities in Britain.
Credit: Karen Robinson/Format

are further examples of alternative modes of state policing and punishment which have **penalising effects** on poor and excluded individuals and groups – notably, social security claimants, lone mothers, visible ethnic minorities, the young and the homeless (see Chapters 5 and 7). These examples demonstrate that not all individuals who are penalised by the state have committed a crime against it.

An alternative way of looking at the relationship between poverty, crime and punishment has been offered in this book. Although the diagramatic representation of these alternative relationships (see Model 2 in Figure 8.1) is in itself over-simplified, it nonetheless exposes the fallacy of the causal, linear view by presenting an altogether more complicated picture.

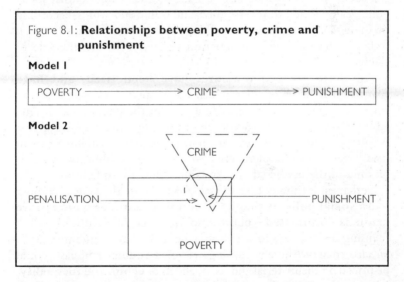

Figure 8.1: **Relationships between poverty, crime and punishment**

Model 1

POVERTY ⟶ CRIME ⟶ PUNISHMENT

Model 2

CRIME

PENALISATION ⟶ PUNISHMENT

POVERTY

Crime is represented here as an 'unknown quantity', as is the less tangible concept of 'penalisation', whereas we can quantify the extent of formal state punishment through the courts and at the end point of the prison. Formal punishment is largely reserved for those poorer groups who constitute the 'identikit prisoner'. As Chapters 3, 4 and 5 demonstrated, the non-poor are formally punished to a far less extent than their poorer counterparts and they are also less liable to suffer from various forms of state penalisation (for example, through the welfare policing) discussed in Chapters 5 and 7. As a result, the poor suffer more in terms of both:

- 'hard' and 'soft' policing; *and*
- judicial punishment and broader (social and welfare) penalisation.

SOCIAL POLICY AND CRIME – TURNING THE TABLES

Those who define the crime agenda in terms of the crimes of the poor do not hesitate to **blame social policy for creating the conditions** (moral, social and economic) under which crime is committed. Consequently, it is argued, personal taxation, welfare, education and immigration policies are causes of the demoralisation and social disorder which lead to rising crime. It follows that social policy can be used to reverse the trend – in other words, according to these views, the reversal of these 'progressive' taxation, social welfare, education and immigration policies will turn the tide of crime.

All these reversal measures have been tried, and have simply not worked: the return to 'Victorian values', 'back to basics', tax cuts for the rich, benefit cuts for the poor, school league tables, moral crusades against single mothers, the Child Support Agency, proposals for divorce law reform and draconian immigration laws have all been implemented – crime rates stubbornly refuse to respond in the predicted (and sustained) downward fashion.

Perhaps it is time to turn the tables and to use the same argument – that **social policies shape the conditions under which more crime is committed** – but to employ it very differently. Instead of focusing on the ways in which social policies have combined to *demoralise* society (thereby causing crime), a counter emphasis could be placed on the material and social effects of **economic inequality**. I have argued that these inequalities generate a context in which crime is more likely to be committed – by rich and poor alike (Chapters 2 and 3). It follows that the social and fiscal policies described in this book (Chapters 2, 5 and 7) which have favoured the rich and disfavoured the poor could be reversed: in this way social policy *could* be employed very differently as a tool to reduce crime.

But this approach would involve mustering the political will to try policy solutions which are beyond the bounds of the criminal justice system itself. This means coming to terms with some politically unpalatable facts about that system, namely that:

- prison does not 'work' to combat crime;
- the police cannot 'solve' the crime problem;
- the criminal justice system does not do justice to all.

The need to accept these fundamentals, and to go beyond the criminal justice system to tackle crime, is precisely what is suggested by David Downes. But this does pose a major political challenge.

> The main priorities for crime prevention and control concern measures which are not in themselves crime-specific. They are problems that need to be tackled by any new government as priorities in their own right: on jobs, on housing, on education and on inequality which, in combination, would amount to the second major era of social reconstruction since 1945.[4]

Bearing in mind the scale of the Labour Party's 1997 election victory, comparisons with the election landslide and the subsequent social reconstruction of 1945 are inevitable. The New Labour government faces enormous challenges and equally enormous opportunities. In CPAG's pre-election publication, *Britain Divided*,[5] Carey Oppenheim identified four principal challenges:

- the legacy of two decades of widening social inequality and growing social deprivation;
- the likely persistence of many of the broader economic and social factors which partly generated those inequalities;
- tight controls on public spending; *and*
- ambiguous public attitudes to paying higher taxes to finance public spending.

At the same time, the parallel opportunities are to:

- seize the chance to 'weld the economic and social together', as policies to combat poverty will lead to greater social cohesion and will benefit society as a whole;
- combat social exclusion by rebuilding individual and community assets;
- broaden the notion of redistribution to include transferring skills (through education), shifting resources between generations and localities as well as between individuals;
- begin to imaginatively put the 'election sensitive' issue of taxation back on the political agenda.

In his first pronouncement as Prime Minister on the steps of 10 Downing Street, Tony Blair promised 'practical measures in pursuit of noble causes'. While social justice is clearly *the* noble cause celèbre, it is significant that he also stressed that 'We were elected as New Labour and we will govern as New Labour.' For some political commentators (such as Hugo Young) there is a danger that this statement may denote a policy of 'cautious centrism which promises only limited results'.[6] But if the challenges of combating the legacy of the past 18 years of social divisions are to be faced, and if the opportunities for building a 'new settlement' for both criminal and social justice are to be grasped, cautious centrism is not enough. Clearly neither politicians nor the electorate wish to replicate the political dogmatism of the past 18 years. But, as Labour elder statesman (and former Deputy Leader) Roy Hattersley tellingly commented, ultimately the electorate will need 'an ideal to live by ... conscience must take precedence over consensus'. Currently, there is the danger that

> Tony Blair has built a government which is untainted by dogma. He is taking the politics out of politics.[7]

While pragmatism may be the watchword for New Labour social policy, it is crucial that there are clearly stated ideals, or at least principles, which are held to **underpin** this apparently fluid policy stance: the problem with pragmatism, as Roy Hattersley perceptively notes, is that 'nobody ever died for it'.[8]

It is very significant that Blair's Southwark speech (2 June 1997) which launched the policies geared to combating poverty was titled '**The Will to Win**'. Despite the rhetoric of 'one nation' and the commitment to forge 'an alliance between the haves and the have nots', this speech stressed that 'you only get out if you put in ... that's the bargain'. Moreover, in education as elsewhere, Blair indicated there would be 'zero tolerance of failure'. It is, therefore, unclear exactly what (in policy terms) is meant by 'social justice' under New Labour. And so long as **social justice** remains a vague and undefined aspiration, it cannot effectively act as a **driver for positive change in social (and criminal justice) policy**.

WHERE TO START?

As the quotation at the opening of this book demonstrated, Jack Straw (now Home Secretary) does not feel we can, in political terms, 'have everything at once' and he has signalled the need to combat social disorder as the main priority in New Labour's crime agenda. In Blair's terms, this may well be tough on crime, but what about being tough on its causes? While awaiting the (promised) social reconstruction, and the 'jobs, and decent housing' which people deserve and need, what should we do about **poverty, crime and punishment**?

We could try to make the criminal justice system operate in a way which would do less harm (and even, maybe, more good), to those who are processed through it. We know what does *not* work – prison and, for young people, punishment-based programmes such as 'shock incarceration, intense surveillance and home confinement'.[9] So much for New Labour youth crime policies, which are predicated on swift and stricter punishment of persistent offenders, curfews and parental responsibility orders.

The findings of the Audit Commission report, *Misspent Youth*,[10] support the view that youth justice policy has not been driven by rational strategy, but by political rhetoric. Consequently it is costly and inefficient in reducing youth crime.[11] Alternative policies would entail social investment to reduce the *risks* associated with offending. According to the Audit Commission, individual case work interventions (which have been seen to fail) should be minimised, whereas the family, the school and the locality offer better opportunities for productive action. Similarly, leisure, education and training opportunities and locally co-ordinated multi-agency approaches to preventing and tackling crime (and drug and alcohol abuse) are all seen to present better chances of success.

This brings us back to the need to **firmly couple social justice and criminal justice – to combat the conditions of poverty and social exclusion which are sources of crime**. At the same time, this social justice based approach would involve policing and punishing the crimes of the rich with a vigour comparable to that directed at the crimes of the poor, and in proportion to the relative threat that each poses to our society.

At the very least we should ensure that social policy and penal policy are working in the same direction. As Barbara Hudson clearly states:

... penal policy is bound to have some effect, for good or ill, on social justice ... A straw is just a straw, but penal policy ought to ensure it is removing straws from the camel's back of inequality, rather than adding to them.[12]

To use another analogy, if criminal and social justice are at either end of a two-way street, then we need to manage the traffic much more sensibly. We must also have a strategy, and the resources, to work efficiently to clear the wreckage – which is caused by poverty, by crime, and by punishment – from *both* ends of that street.

NOTES

1 J Reiman, *The Rich Get Rich and the Poor Get Prison*, Macmillan, 1990.
2 D Rose, *In the Name of the Law*, Jonathan Cape, 1996.
3 Barbara Amiel, *Sunday Times* 24 April 1994, quoted in *ibid*, p336.
4 D Downes, 'What the next government should do about crime', in *The Howard Journal*, Vol 36, No 1, 1997, p11.
5 C Oppenheim, 'The growth of poverty and inequality', in A Walker and C Walker (eds), *Britain Divided: the growth of social exclusion in the 1980s and 1990s*, CPAG Ltd, 1997, p28.
6 *Guardian*, 3 May 1997.
7 *Guardian*, 14 May 1997.
8 *Ibid*.
9 Audit Commission, *Misspent Youth: young people and crime*, Audit Commission, 1996.
10 *Ibid*.
11 *Ibid*.
12 B Hudson, *Penal Policy and Social Justice*, Macmillan, 1993, p15.

APPENDIX ONE

SOCIAL DEPRIVATION INDICES

Census variables used in computing deprivation indices
(shading indicates variables used by a given index)

	Deprivation Index			
Variable	Carstairs	DoE Z	Townsend	Jarman
Unemployment		■	■	■
Male unemployment	■			
Overcrowding	■	■	■	
No access to car	■	■	■	
Single parent families		■		■
Pensioners living alone		■		■
Not owner-occupiers			■	
Ethnic minorities		■		■
Lack of amenities		■		
Young children				■
Low social class	■	■		
Recent migrants				■

What deprivation indices are trying to measure

Index	General field	Description
Carstairs	Deprivation	'Reflects people's access to material resources – a dimension from affluence to poverty – reflects wealth and income'
DoE Z	Needs assessment	'To inform the allocation of resources to local authorities'
Townsend	Material deprivation	'The material apparatus, goods, services, resources, amenities and physical environment and location of life'
Jarman	Underprivilege	'Factors affecting demand for GP services; needs for primary care'

Adapted from V Carstairs, 'Overview of deprivation indices', in N Spencer and H Janes (eds), *Uses and abuses of deprivation indices*, University of Warwick, 1992.

APPENDIX TWO

A NOTE ON 'ETHNIC MINORITY' CLASSIFICATIONS

1 The Wolverhampton Crime Audit involved the comparison of locally collected data on crimes and victims (provided by the West Midlands Police force) and a variety of supplementary data, including 1991 Census data, BCS data and Wolverhampton Council research.

2 The BCS 1988 and 1992 surveys used categories of ethnicity from the 1991 Census, but the 'ethnic booster sample' used the following terms (as the number of respondents from smaller ethnic groups were insufficient for further study):

- Afro-Caribbean (defined as 'blacks' of African, Caribbean or other origin);
- Asian (defined as those of Indian, Pakistani or Bangladeshi origin).

3 The Wolverhampton Poverty Study used the term 'Black' to refer to all those respondents who **classified themselves** as Black African, Black Caribbean or Black other.

4 By contrast, self-classification is not involved in the collection of victim data by the West Midlands Police: police data is based on officers' perception of ethnic origin and uses categories based largely on appearance and skin colour, namely:

- White European;
- Dark European;
- Afro-Caribbean;
- Asian;
- Oriental;
- Arabian.

5 The analysis of victim data modified the categories used by the West Midlands Police in order to enable comparison with both national and other regional sets of data. The categories used were:

- White (including 'European');
- Black (including 'Black African, Black Afro-Caribbean and Black "other"');
- Asian (including all those of 'Indian, Pakistani and Bangladeshi origin');
- Other.